Marketing Matters

The Ultimate Reference Guide To Making
the Most Of your Marketing Money

By Harvey Goldglantz

D1496206

PMP books

Printed in the United States of America

ISBN 978-0-9790542-1-1

Published by PMP Books, a division of Questex Media Group

Questex Media Group is a U.S. business information company that publishes magazines and journals, produces expositions and conferences and provides a range of marketing services.

Book Design: RJ Pooch
Project Managers: Frank Andorka and Jamie Kleist
Book Printer: Bang Printing, Brainerd, MN

Dedication

I dedicate this book to my wife, Gayle, who is my compass:
For her wisdom, her guidance, her support, her intellect,
her unshakable confidence and her love.

Her strength, perseverance and incredible kindness have made
this world a better place for all of us.

I admire, respect, value and love her even more today than I
did when I said "I do" more than 37 years ago.

Contents

Foreword

My introduction to marketing began early on, when I was a small child growing up in Mount Airy, a northwest section of the greater Philadelphia area.

I did not understand it then, but I would ultimately come to the realization that my entire life experience, as a marketing and business consultant, was being formed and shaped since that time.

During the early to mid-1950s, my grandparents owned a small Army-Navy store in Penns Grove, N.J. On the weekends and during the summer, I can recall visiting with them, probably from around the age of four or five, and helping them arrange the display windows of their store so that they would attract customers as they passed by. My grandmother would lovingly guide my hand with a Magic Marker and help me design signs that would be placed on top of the merchandise racks.

During the mid-1950s, my parents purchased a women's dress shop in North Philadelphia, where my "education" in marketing, merchandising, business and sales continued to develop into my early teens.

I can vividly recall interacting with customers, watching intently as my parents designed newspaper ads and offering my mostly ignored suggestions on Saturdays and during the summertime. I loved working at their store — and the extra allowance didn't hurt, either.

Then tragedy struck for the first time, in July 1963. My mother died of breast cancer. It struck again, a few years later, when my father succumbed to a heart attack, leaving myself and my brother orphaned. I had instantly become the head of the household.

At my father's funeral, a distant cousin approached and offered me a part-time job at his pest control company. He said that if I accepted, he would make sure that I would be able to earn enough money to continue to support my household, which consisted of my brother, myself and our grandmother (my father's mother), who was 90 and had been living with us for a number of years.

This is where the story and my "education" takes many twists and turns.

I went to work for my cousin's pest control company, working after school, on the weekends and during the summertime. During the week, my job consisted of calling customers, setting up appointments, selling on the phone, composing scripts and doing anything and everything necessary to generate business.

On the weekends, I learned how to be a technician. By my third weekend on the street, I was generating more production, referrals and sales than anyone else in the company, including my cousin, using creative marketing and sales strategies that I had learned while working for my parents and grandparents. At that time, I put together my first strategic plan, which consisted of two major goals: Support my family and earn enough money to put myself through college. I succeeded at both.

During that first summer working for my cousin's company, I noticed that on Saturdays, Philadelphia closed a percentage of streets to allow for street-cleaning by the neighbors. The city distributed trash bags, brooms, paint,

flower planters and other beautification tools to targeted neighborhoods.

I should note that Philadelphia is comprised mostly of attached row homes. On average, there are 100 homes per street. Fifty homes are located on each side of the street. Each home was approximately 1,000 square feet, and consisted of three levels: a basement, the first-floor living area and the second-floor bedrooms and bathroom.

My cousin considered these street closings as a great inconvenience and hindrance to his productivity because it meant he would have to navigate around the closed streets to get to his customers.

I, however, wondered to myself whether there was any pattern to these street closings. If there was, how could I find out which streets would be closed and on what days? How many streets were closed? In what neighborhoods? Is there a contact person on each street? I decided to take a trip to City Hall one day after school to see whether I could discover some untapped market potential for myself.

I will never forget that day.

As I approached the front desk of the Streets Department, my palms were sweating. Would anyone speak with me? After all, I was just a gawky teenager. What could I use as a hook to catch my bait? Then it came to me like a bolt of lightning: I had my sales (marketing) pitch.

"Good morning, my name is Harvey Goldglantz, and I would very much like to help the neighbors clean up the streets of the city during my summer break."

"That's very nice of you, young man," the woman at the desk responded.

I continued, "I was wondering if there is a listing of the streets that are to be closed each week."

"Oh yes," she replied. "Would you like me to provide you with a printout?"

"That would be terrific," I said. "Is there a name of a person, on each street, that I can contact to let them know I am coming?"

"Oh yes," she replied. "There is a block captain for every street, and I will include their names and phone numbers on your list."

I left City Hall that day with a couple hundred sheets of paper, listing all of the street closings by date and neighborhood for the next year. The list also included the names, addresses and phone numbers of the individual block captains.

I've hit pay dirt, I thought. And as you will soon discover, that was an understatement. But remember, I was still working for my cousin's pest control company (at least for the next week).

I went home that evening and decided that I needed to develop a marketing pitch that would make it a win-win situation: for myself, the block captains and the potential customers that lived on each street.

The Pitch

"*Hello, Mrs. _____, my name is Harvey Goldglantz and I'm with Philadelphia Exterminating Company.*" I made up this name. I figured that it sounded like a large company.

"*I understand that your street is closed for street cleaning on _____ and that you are the block captain. We are going to have one of our trucks in your neighborhood*

that day, and we'll do any home from the basement to the upstairs for only $5, and it's completely guaranteed." I didn't have a truck, but that was just a detail.

"If you provide us with a list of homes that are interested in our services, we will give you 10% of every initial service visit."

The result of making that first call to a block captain resulted in 62 out of 100 of the row homes requesting service on that first Saturday.

Needless to say, I gave my notice to my cousin that first week.

But I realized, during my first job, that there was more gold to be had in "them thar hills." I learned two important lessons from my parents, grandparents and cousin:

Lesson #1: Repeat business (customer retention) is directly related to growth and profitability.

Lesson #2: Look for opportunities to sell additional goods and services (add-ons).

And so, during my *first day of sales* as a company "owner," my revenue looked like this:

62 homes @ $5/home (initial service)
30 homes @ $10/home (additional rodent service)
40 homes @$10/home (two months' advance deposit on annual monthly service contract
$1,010 Gross
-$31   Commission to block captain on initial service
$979 Net

By my third week in business, I employed two firemen in addition to myself and was grossing almost $3,000 on a Saturday. Not bad for a kid in his mid-teens in the 1960s.

I am sure that you will agree that based on the above example, creative marketing worked and was well worth the effort.

It doesn't matter if it was pest control or some other service- or product-based business. Where there is a will, there is a way.

By my late teens, I was well on my way to having my college education paid for and then some.

However, I still was uncertain about what career path to head down. I decided to major in communications and marketing, and graduated from Temple University in 1971.

During my college years, while still running my pest control business on Saturdays and during the summertime, I was fortunate to land a job at a local television station, which ultimately became the Fox affiliate in Philadelphia. I began my stint as a production assistant and was eventually offered the job of executive producer of a TV local talk show upon graduation. I declined and realized that if I wanted to earn a good living (which I already was), there were other venues that offered larger opportunities.

Upon graduation, I applied for a job as assistant to the president of a multimillion-dollar retail company in center city Philadelphia, while still running my pest control business on Saturdays and during the summer. Of course, by that time I had incorporated the name Philadelphia Exterminating Co., and hired a manager and additional employees.

While working for this large retail company, at the ripe old age of 22, I was responsible for the oversight and administration of a $300,000 advertising and marketing budget — as well as being ultimately accountable for overall store sales and growth. I eventually became involved in all facets of the business and its administration.

I worked for the company for approximately three years, and was successful in convincing them to open up branches in New Jersey and Delaware. I worked feverishly to help them develop and solidify their brand. Our media mix included directory advertising, TV, radio and direct mail.

I still was overseeing my pest management business, but now had a full-time manager and a staff that could handle the increasing workload. But I still wasn't certain that this was my career of choice.

Two things then happened simultaneously during 1974. First, a representative from a Big Six accounting firm had heard about the success that I had running the retail business and with my own pest management company. He asked me whether I would be interested in doing some per-diem consulting work for some of their retail and service accounts that were having some problems. I accepted, and I was successful in putting together some strategic marketing and business plans that took them from being on the brink to being profitable organizations.

Second, I was contacted by the past Chairman of the Board of a national retail sweater and shirt manufacturer and was asked to help him open a retail men's and women's clothing factory outlet. I would be responsible for all facets of the organization, including developing the brand, marketing the brand and the oversight of a potential multimillion dollar business. I was 25 years old at the time. I accepted.

Once again, I was back in the retail clothing business.

But ultimately, the decision was made for me. One week before I got married in 1971, we discovered that my wife, Gayle, had end-stage renal disease. The doctors told us to enjoy our honeymoon because when we returned she would have to go on dialysis. Fortunately, for us, their prediction did not come to pass for another five years. Gayle began dialysis in 1976.

At that time we were told that the average end-stage renal patient lived two years without a transplant. Dialysis during the 1970s meant visits to the hospital three times per week until a transplant could be found. At that point, I realized that scheduling and flexibility would become the most important components in my career.

I left the 9-to-5 jobs in the dust and pursued a two-tiered career: Business owner and consultant.

I am happy to report that both marketing and medicine have come a long way in the past 37 years. After 12 years on and off dialysis, a bout with cancer and four kidney transplants, Gayle continues to enjoy a quality of life well beyond anyone's original expectations.

Approximately five years ago, I sold my pest management business to one of my consulting clients and finally decided to

devote the balance of my career to one of the two loves in my life: marketing and business consulting.

I have worked for clients in many diverse industries during my career, from the retail trade to the wholesale trade, from manufacturing to the service industries. The companies for which I have worked have ranged in size from start-ups to companies with annual revenues in excess of $30 million.

I am writing this book from the unique perspective of having melded my experiences from childhood, along with my education, experiences as a business owner, as an executive with two large companies, as an independent consultant for a Big Six accounting firm, a columnist for a nationally recognized industry magazine for 15 years (*Pest Management Professional*) and finally as an independent business and marketing consultant.

This book will look at marketing from many different perspectives, but will always keep growth and profitability at the forefront of any consideration or recommendation.

It matters not whether you are an electrician, a retailer, a pest management professional, a lawn care company owner, a manufacturer, a supplier or hotel owner. The principles that you will discover in this book are universal. The lessons to be learned will lead you to the conclusion that a well planned marketing strategy must be incorporated into your strategic planning if you are to achieve consistent growth.

It all begins with a vision.

chapter 1
The Big Picture

Any man can see farther than he can reach, but that doesn't mean that he should quit reaching. It all begins with a clear vision.

As I grew up, it became clear to me that in order to rise above the crowd, it was necessary to strive. Being content with what is may work for some, but in order to achieve, I realized that reaching paved the path to potential success.

Although historical perspective is a prerequisite for prudent planning, vision must accompany it if great success is to be achieved.

What separates great success from mediocrity is vision.

Three Visionaries
Sam Walton:
The Consummate Retail Merchandiser
Sam Walton built his multibillion-dollar business based upon a vision. That vision evolved from a single store in Bentonville, Ark.: Walton's Five and Dime. The small mom-and-pop corner store ultimately became the largest retail organization in the world: Wal-Mart. Sam Walton's vision was unique and would have a far-reaching impact on the world of retailing. It included viewing his managers as "servant leaders." This concept of service management reached far into the communities that Wal-Mart served.

"Each Wal-Mart store should reflect the values of its customers and support the vision they hold for their community," Walton once said.

Walton's strategic marketing plan and operating focus centered on becoming one with the community. He urged his managers to join local Rotary Clubs and other civic organizations. He invited community groups into his stores to hold bake sales and other fundraising events.

Walton also pioneered the concept of discount merchandising, focusing on volume sales by working on small mark-ups and slim profit margins. This was a revolutionary concept in the 1960s.

Walton's operating focus included the following directives, as the company grew and expanded:

• On Monday through Thursday, senior executives were to travel to stores all over the country, watching, listening and talking to customers and employees.

• On Friday, the executives were to return to Bentonville to meet with the company's merchandise managers.

• On Saturdays, there would be a management meeting in Bentonville. Top managers from around the country were invited to attend. At times, more than 1,000 managers and executives were present.

• There would be a conscious effort to maintain a family atmosphere and a sense of fulfillment among its employees.

• To become a manager, you must maintain an attitude of learning, listening and teaching.

• The operating strategy would be people-driven, and the managers would be agents for the customer.

• Comprehensive training programs would be implemented at all levels.

• The company would be mission-focused, value-based and demographically driven.

• The company would exchange operating information with a select group of non-competing companies to enhance its own marketing position.

Scott Cook:
An Icon of the Software Industry

Scott Cook is probably a name that you are not familiar with, but I am quite certain that you are familiar with his multi-billion-dollar company, Intuit — creator of Quicken and QuickBooks.

Cook graduated with an MBA from the Harvard Business School in 1976. Upon graduation, he went to work for Proctor and Gamble, where he learned about product development, market research and marketing.

In the early 1980s, he left P&G after recognizing the potential of the personal computer market and realizing the need for a software program to help people pay their bills. In 1983, he launched Intuit and the rest, shall we say, is history.

Legend has it that his company began in the basement of his home, with an idea and a developing vision.

Cook learned at Harvard and at P&G that if he was to be successful, listening to his customers would be the key to his success. Too few companies heed that important advice today, but Intuit's success was built on it.

Once his initial personal financial software program was developed, Cook needed to test its functionality and marketability. Hence, he initiated Intuit's "Follow Me Home" program.

Cook had one of his employees visit a local computer store, where the software was being sold on a test basis.

The employee watched as a customer purchased the product and then asked whether he could accompany them home and observe their interaction with the product.

The Intuit employee watched closely as the customer interacted with the product. No detail went unchecked. Every frustration, pause and interaction between the customer and the software was closely observed — from the opening of the packaging to the ease or difficulty of navigating the program.

Why such attention to detail? Because Cook knew that if his software program was to be successful on a mass scale, it would have to be more convenient and easier to use than picking up a pen, writing a check and recording the transaction. After numerous observations by his employees of customer interactions with the software, Cook began his initial thrust toward mass marketing.

Works for Quicken

Initially, Cook had hired only two sales representatives to market his product. However, he quickly discovered that the software was selling itself. Wherever the software was being sold, purchasers were spreading the word about its value and ease of use. After being on the market for only a short period, Cook was overheard saying to an employee, "We have hundreds of thousands of potential salespersons: They're our customers."

WOM

Referral program

Cook's vision encompassed focusing on marketing research, design and customer service. His original operating focus, marketing plan, objectives and methodology included some of the following strategies:

• The company will do continuing quality assurance surveys, asking customers what they need and want — then develop the programs to meet their needs.

• The company will offer free technical support.

• The customer should be able to learn the software in six minutes or it's free.

• The customer should feel so good

follow-ups - phone calls

about the product that they spread the word.

- Thank-you letters from customers will be read aloud to employees and circulated throughout the company, then framed and posted on the wall.
- The company will call customers to make sure they are happy.
- Virtually every employee in the company has to spend some time every month working the customer service lines.
- Every few months, each employee will be taken to lunch by a senior manager.
- A torrent of statistics tracking the company's performance will be displayed on the wall.
- Customer-service systems will be reviewed at all meetings prior to financials.
- The company will be structured to encourage cooperation and to make improvements through innovation, rather than by implementing tighter controls.
- Employees will not get extra compensation for additional hours worked, but will participate in profit-sharing.
- The company will implement a media advertising campaign based on the following copy: "Send for a copy of Quicken. Pay only $8 for shipping and handling. If you don't think you're doing useful work within a few minutes, don't pay for the product."

Alvin "Bugs" Burger: An Innovator in the Service Sector

In 1960, Alvin Burger and his wife, Sandee, began their Miami-based "exterminating" company with $300 in borrowed money and a dream. By 1986, when Burger sold his nationally renowned pest management business to S.C. Johnson Wax, the company was grossing a reported $30 million a year.

Bugs Burger Bug Killers, or BBBK as it had come to be known, had by that time expanded into 44 states and had 15,000 hotel and restaurant accounts. Burger's vision was unique, innovative, trend-setting and made heads turn. While his competitors focused on pest management, with the goal of elimination, Burger's concept and guarantee promised total pest elimination or your money back... and more.

With this revolutionary marketing offer and guarantees, Burger targeted the hospitality and restaurant industries. He would soon discover that his originality, combined with his vision and operational focus was about to set his industry abuzz and make him a wealthy man. He achieved many firsts.

The BBBK Guarantees

Initially, Burger's competitors thought he was crazy and scoffed at his "extreme" ideas. They wanted to know how Burger could make these promises and still expect to stay in business, let alone make a profit. It was all in his vision, operational focus and methodology — his master plan.

The secret to BBBK's success resulted from the following strategic planning:

- It went after a targeted market: high-end hospitality and restaurant segments. These were large accounts that could both afford and value this extraordinary service.
- It made a unique original offer (his guarantees) that would entice potential accounts to purchase his services.
- It revolutionized the guarantee in the pest management industry. In actuality,

they were not only selling pest elimination, but were also offering an insurance policy (risk reduction). The guarantee gave their customers peace of mind, and in their minds transferred the risk from the customer to the service provider (insurer).

• For this marketing strategy to be successful, it would have to be backed up through scrupulous operational focus and execution. All support systems had to be operating at close to 100 percent, for the cost of mistakes would go directly to the bottom line.

• It made the client equally responsible for keeping the guarantees in force by increasing the frequency of clean-ups, changing its trash-disposal procedures or making BBBK-specified repairs. Client cooperation was mandatory, and the customer had a clearly acknowledged responsibility to perform. This duality of client/company responsibility was a critical part in keeping the guarantee.

• The conditions of the guarantees were clearly defined and specified in unambiguous terms. What the big print gives, the small print takes away.

• The company charged accounts up to 10 times more than its competitors. Normally, you would figure that this type of price differential would be a deterrent. In actuality, just the opposite proved to be true. The clients were so overwhelmed

---

The B.B.B.K Guarantees

Guaranteed Performance

1. You do not pay our initial charges until we totally eliminate every roach, rat or mouse nesting on your premises.

2. If you're ever dissatisfied with our results and want to cancel our service we will:

   A. Refund up to one year's service charge.

   B. Pay the cost of another exterminator of your choice for one year.

Guaranteed Protection

1. Should a roach or rodent be seen by one of your guests, we will pay their bill*, send them a letter of apology and invite them back as our guest.

2. We will pay all fines that may be levied against your hotel by the health authorities for the presence of roaches or rodents.

3. Should your hotel or restaurant ever be closed by the health authorities for the presece of roaches or rodents, "Bugs" Burger will pay profits lost while you are closed, plus $5,000.

*Hotel Rooms - One Room Night

---

by the guarantee and the prospect of total pest elimination that they saw great value in the offer. Remember, we are talking about the hospitality and restaurant industries, where the sight of pests could mean the permanent loss of recurring revenue.

• The company put into place proactive and comprehensive training programs.

• It also developed a comprehensive inspection and quality control program.

• It initiated and implemented a proactive hiring program that identified prospective employees who would be committed to its philosophy and core values.

• It recognized the value of its employees through extraordinary compensation offerings.

• It displayed a willingness to fire customers that did not comply with its recommendations.

Yes, it all began with a vision by these three industry icons. But vision alone did not bring them success. That came with the inclusion of six key business principles, which I refer to as the Six Golden Keys that open the doors to success.

Key #1: Thought

It all begins with an idea, a thought. We think about how we want to accomplish something. For some, it may come in the form of daydreaming. For others, ideas may come to us in that twilight time just before we nod off to sleep. We never know just when or were that pearl of wisdom will come from, but one thing is for certain: Unless we write it down, it may be as fleeting as a gust of wind.

Rule #1: Keep a pad and pen by your side at all times to capture those great ideas.

Key #2: Planning

Thoughts by themselves have no legs unless they are put into the form of a written strategic plan. Begin with an outline of what you want to accomplish. What are your goals? Then specifically state how you are going to accomplish them. What methodology will you use? How much revenue do you expect the idea to bring in? What are your cost projections? As part of the planning process, you should create a budget.

Rule #2: Put together a comprehensive written plan, accompanied by a budget.

Key #3: Execution

I am certain that you are aware of the proverb "The best-laid plans of mice and men often go astray." Great thoughts and outstanding plans often go nowhere without implementation. It is imperative that you put into place the appropriate personnel that will carry out your directives.

Rule #3: Have the right people on board whom you can trust to execute your plans.

Key #4: Follow-Through

Even if your plans are executed perfectly initially, you must make certain that your strategies are followed as the plan progresses. Therefore, it is imperative to have quality control systems in place that constantly monitor the plan's status.

Rule #4: Establish quality control systems to monitor the plan's progress.

Key #5: Change

Be flexible. As market conditions change, you must be willing to adapt accordingly and move quickly. If you take too long to respond to unforeseen circumstances, your once-"brilliant" plan may become obsolete quickly.

Rule #5: Be willing to change and rethink strategies as market conditions require.

Key #6: Chance

Even with a great deal of thought, planning, execution, follow-through and flexibility, you are still not guaranteed success unless you are willing to take risk. This is the final quality that Walton, Cook and Burger had in common. They were each willing to put their dollars where their visions were. They were willing to invest in themselves. This quality of putting it all on the line for what you believe in is a trait that all great entre-

preneurs and success stories share. This is, perhaps, the most important ingredient of all for great success.

Rule #6: Prudent risk-taking is as important to success as air is to breathing.

To best demonstrate, in everyday terms, how the above model works, I would like to use an example taken from a typical, hypothetical family experience:

Let's say that you are married and have two young daughters. Your vision is that they will grow up to be happy, healthy and prosperous young women. You know that they will need plenty of help and guidance along the way throughout the years. You think, early on, about all of their needs growing up and about how you will assist in fulfilling them. But just thinking about it will not make it happen. So, you begin planning early on in their childhoods about how to meet these needs.

You project what their needs will be along the way: health insurance, food, clothing, education, a wedding (or two), etc. You prepare financially for what you will need to get them through: a life insurance policy, medical insurance, money for their educations and weddings. But planning alone will not cut it unless you begin putting money away early (execution of the plan).

A bump or two in the road comes along. You may not realize it, but pretty soon you are behind in your savings plan. That is why it is important to revisit your plan from time to time to make certain that it is still on target (follow-through).

Then, all of a sudden, an unexpected expense comes along: One of your daughters gets accepted to medical school. You must then be willing to modify (change)

your plan to make certain that you have enough resources available for your other child.

Finally, sometimes during the course of your lifetime, you may just have to take a chance to make it all come together. That is just part of life. No pain, no gain. No risk, no reward. Same as business.

Most business owners and managers would never acknowledge this, but in my opinion the marketing portion of the business never quite receives the time, depth of consideration or respect that it deserves.

Most executives use the terms "marketing" and "advertising" almost interchangeably. While advertising is one component of marketing, it is only one component. Marketing also includes innumerable other pieces of the business puzzle.

When marketing is viewed from an all-inclusive perspective, its "totality of value" becomes much greater than the sum of its individual parts. On page 8, you will find a diagram that includes the various topics that are included in this book. I did this in the shape of a puzzle for a few specific reasons:

First, I wanted you to be able to see just how many facets of your business fall under the influence of marketing. It is actually quite remarkable. From the design of your invoices to your vehicle signage (if you are a service company, retailer or wholesaler), from your strategic planning to caring for your employees, it's all marketing. From your advertising to your pricing and sales force — you guessed it, marketing…marketing… marketing.

Second, I want you to focus on the chart on page 8 again for a moment.

Look how interrelated all the pieces of the puzzle are to one another. Each piece is held firmly in place by an adjoining piece. When one part of the puzzle comes unglued, the entire foundation becomes a little bit weaker.

By reading through this book, I hope that you will come to the realization that planning your marketing strategy in advance is as important as every other facet of your business, and maybe more important than most.

I have written this book from the perspective of a businessperson who has a strong background in marketing. In actuality, I spend as much time consulting with companies on general business issues as I do consulting on marketing strategies.

I have tried to include all the major marketing themes in this book. I believe that you will find it a useful reference book for years to come.

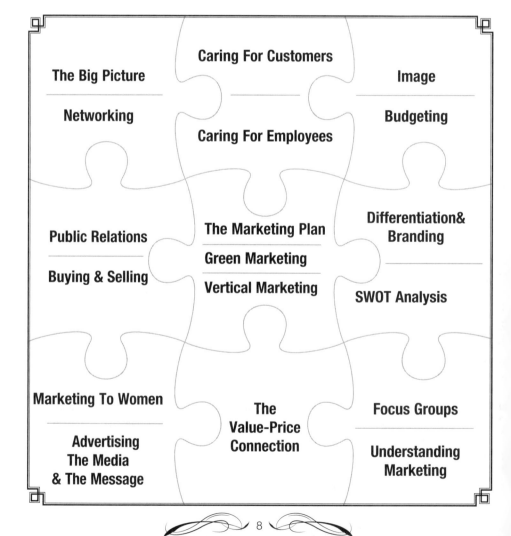

My goal for you is to kick that ball — the marketing plan that you will develop after reading this book — through the goalpost, and achieve all of your own personal business goals while you're at it.

That's not to say that there won't be fumbles. There will be. But learn from them and do things better the next time. You must analyze and correct your mistakes and build on your accomplishments.

Football actually brings to mind a number of business analogies. I would like to share just a few with you before you delve further into this book.

• A business is like a football team. It encompasses commitment, planning, investment, organization, competition and a unified team approach.

• You must clearly define your game plan.

• Just because you were successful before is no guarantee that your success will continue unless you constantly plan, review, adapt and change.

• You must be able to motivate your team to accomplish your goals.

• You must be willing to implement change, taking calculated risks, to move the ball forward.

• You may get pushed back by the competition from time to time, but you must be able to regroup and find a more successful way of outmaneuvering them the next time.

• The object of the game of football is to score the most points. The object of the game of business is to wind up with the most profit.

As you proceed through the balance of this book, you will note that the chapters begin at a relatively relaxed pace, with simple concepts, and methodically and

progressively expand to more in-depth subject matter with much greater detail. This is by conscious design.

It is my purpose to draw you in slowly, making my case so to speak, to get you to want to move on to the next chapter. I figured that once the train began moving and picking up speed, you would be anxious to go from stop chapter) to stop (chapter), in anticipation of reaching your final destination: marketing enlightenment.

chapter 2
Caring for Your Customers

With a clear vision in hand, accompanied by a full set of "keys" (I am referring to the Six Golden Keys in the previous chapter), successful companies are able to construct and clearly define customer service strategies that complement and support their business models. Doing so allows them to use this policy as a marketing tool — and an invaluable strategic asset.

Customer care is a philosophy that begins at the top of the company and works its way through the core of the business. It becomes the essence of what a company is.

While almost everyone understands the value and impact of customer care, too few companies are able to translate that understanding into an articulate and actionable service-delivery system and strategic marketing advantage.

Those companies that are successful at delivering, projecting and marketing the customer care concept will have a great competitive benefit over that of their competitors. It doesn't matter if you are selling products or services: Every customer (potential or existing) wants to feel special and valued, and every individual wants to believe that he is receiving value for his investment.

Masters of marketing, like Donald Trump, Las Vegas entrepreneur Steve Wynn, Sam Walton, Southwest Airlines Founder Herb Kelleher, Scott Cook and Bugs Burger, clearly understood that what they were selling first and foremost was perception — and that the projection of a well-conceived perception model is based on the value proposition of a superior service delivery system.

Their ultimate goal was to project the value proposition: By purchasing their service(s), you can be secure in knowing that they were going to exceed your expectations. Therefore, price alone never became the focal point of the sale. Dependability, reputation, trust, knowledge and, of course, quality, became the hallmarks of the value proposition.

The Nordstrom Customer Service Model

Nordstrom, the nationally renowned department store retailer, with locations throughout the United States, became celebrated for setting the standards for outstanding customer service and exceeding customer expectations.

For years they distributed to new hires their employee manual, which consisted of a 5- by 8-inch gray card bearing the following 75 words:

WELCOME TO NORDSTROM

We're glad to have you with our company. Our No. 1 goal is to provide outstanding customer service. Set both your personal and professional goals high. We have great confidence in your ability to achieve them.

Nordstrom Rules:

Rule #1: Use your good judgment in all situations.

There will be no additional rules.

Please feel free to ask your department manager, store manager or division general manager any question at any time.

Today, new hires still receive this card, along with a comprehensive employee manual.

In a nutshell, Nordstrom's philosophy as it pertains to customer service is this: "Do what is right for the customer, and you will have done what's right for the company."

This customer-driven service strategy is reinforced internally at many levels within great companies.

Great companies, with focused core customer service models, follow Nordstrom's lead when it comes to incorporating customer service standards into company culture. These standards, set by Nordstrom, include putting into place the following internal system:

• Senior managers will be responsible for the creation, maintenance and support of customer service-driven programs that sustain the company culture. They will acknowledge, recognize and reward employees who deliver superior customer service. They will also create an atmosphere of helpfulness and professionalism with employees and customers, and educate customers to allow for good decision-making when it comes to product or service selection.

• Supervisors will support and reinforce the position of senior management by hiring the right people, providing ongoing mentoring motivation, and training, acknowledging and rewarding employees for outstanding customer interaction and empowering and encouraging team members.

• Employees must understand, accept and focus on their roles as key elements in the customer service equation, and be focused on building and maintaining these relationships. They must have a complete understanding of the products and services offered and be able to present that information to the customer from a benefits-oriented perspective.

Nordstrom would rather hire pleasant people who are good communicators and teach them to sell, than hire individuals with strong product knowledge and weak people skills. Nordstrom, it's said, "hires the smile and trains the skill." Employees are encouraged to make decisions that always favor the customer and are never criticized for their decisions.

The Nordstrom Customer Service Legend

Nordstrom's customer service delivery system has become legendary. First, the unwritten, absolute satisfaction guaranteed policy states that if for any reason a customer is dissatisfied with a product purchased from a Nordstrom store, it may be returned at any time for a credit or a full refund. Additionally, Nordstrom will never embarrass a customer.

According to company lore, an elderly gentleman thought that he had purchased a set of tires at a local Nordstrom. After noting his dissatisfaction with the product to his wife, he decided to return the tires for a refund. Problem was that Nordstrom never sold tires. Rather than embarrass the elderly gentleman — obviously he was a regular shopper and they knew him — the store manager issued a full credit for what the customer said he paid (since he didn't have a receipt).

Now, that is how the story goes. But true or not, you get the picture of what Nordstrom will do to satisfy a customer. It gives new meaning to the old adage, "The customer is always right."

My Nordstrom Tale

A few years ago, I was in Washington attending a two-day conference. My wife accompanied me and tooled around the nation's capital shopping.

I will never forget that experience.

It was a Sunday afternoon around 6 p.m., and I had just returned from a day of meetings. As I entered my hotel room, my wife was frantic, informing me that she could not find her wallet. We searched the room, to no avail. I asked her if she could remember the last time that she saw it. She recalled taking it out of her handbag, to make a purchase at the makeup counter at Nordstrom in Pentagon City. But she was fairly certain that she placed it back in her handbag after the purchase and that someone probably opened her bag and took it on the Metro trip back from the mall.

The first thing we did was to call Nordstrom security, but the store was closed. The second thing we did was cancel all of the credit cards in her wallet. The third thing we did was call hotel security, and they contacted the police.

When the police arrived, we recounted the story to the officer and he made one of the most incredible statements that I had ever heard.

"Well, Mrs. Goldglantz," he said, "if you lost your wallet at Nordstrom, I am certain that you will get it back."

On Monday morning, around 10 a.m., we contacted Nordstrom security about the lost wallet. They informed us that no one had turned in a woman's wallet. We left our contact information and we were convinced the wallet was gone forever.

At 1 p.m. that afternoon, my cell phone rang. It was the store manager of Nordstrom in Pentagon City. "Mr. Goldglantz, we have your wife's wallet," the voice on the other end of the phone said. "I want to apologize for not calling you sooner, but the sales executive from the cosmetic counter put it in her drawer and only turned it in a few minutes ago."

The manager then went on to inform me that the wallet had a total of eight credit cards, a driver's license and $105 in cash.

I was dumbfounded.

He asked if I was going to pick it up that day. I told him that I was just getting ready to leave Washington for Pennsylvania and asked whether he could mail it COD to my home.

He quickly responded, "I will be happy to mail it to your home FedEx Next Day Delivery, but I wouldn't think of sending it COD. It is our pleasure to pay the freight, and please visit us again soon."

The next morning, back at home in Pennsylvania, the doorbell rang. It was the FedEx driver asking me to sign for an enormous package. Inside the FedEx box was a gold Nordstrom gift box with a gigantic red bow. Inside the gift box was my wife's wallet wrapped in tissue paper, complementary cosmetic samples for her and me, a $100 gift certificate for our "trouble," and a letter of apology from the store manager. Now that's customer service. We were speechless.

Needless to say, my wife and I are now loyal Nordstrom shoppers. Lesson to be learned: Customer Care and Short-Term Sacrifice = Lifetime Customer Loyalty.

Companies that focus on delivering superior customer care understand that the essence of customer service is based on the fostering of personal relationships and the building of credibility. This becomes the foundation of selling any product or service.

To exemplify this, let's look at another example of superb customer service: Southwest Airlines.

For years, while other airlines watched their revenues and profits decline, Southwest Airlines stayed in the black. Why? Great customer service. People know that Southwest Airlines will take them where they want to go, get them there on time, at a competitive price and without losing their luggage to boot. Southwest ownership, management and employees work as a team to facilitate an image of superior customer service and the resultant perception of same.

What Southwest Airlines' employees are first and foremost delivering is the perception of superior customer care. It is one the few airlines — if not the only one — where you will find a relaxed atmosphere among customers and employees. Smiles are commonplace. Southwest Airline employees actually enjoy solving customer problems.

Why are their employees so happy? Simply put: The company understands that they are on the front lines with the customer. According to Colleen Barrett, past president and chief operating officer of Southwest Airlines, "You have to put the customers second…employees are the company's No. 1 customer." Her theory is that if she can effectively make employees feel good about what they're doing, satisfied employees will deliver the same sense of friendliness and care to Southwest passengers.

Want to know how the airline interviews prospective flight attendants? They invite frequent fliers to their offices during the interview process for their input.

Southwest Airline employees are encouraged to express themselves during the day. For those who have traveled the airline, you have probably heard a flight attendant or two burst out in song. On Halloween, employees are encouraged to don costumes. Talk about building relationships.

Now that we have taken a look at how two great companies have built successful customer service models, it is time to assess the customer service delivery system in your own company.

The Three Levels of Customer Service

There are three levels of customer service: The Desired Level of Service, The Adequate Level of Service and The Inadequate Level of Service. Generally, all three levels are operating at once within a business. Hopefully, the inadequate level of service is almost imperceptible, as it represents dissatisfied customers, cancellations and the lack of repeat business.

1) The Desired Level of Service

The desired level of service is that level of service that we all hope to receive, but do not expect. It means going beyond a customer's expectations. Operating at this high level of service fosters customer loyalty, ensures repeat business and increases customer referrals. Of course, it also insulates the company against cancellations.

Some examples of operating at this level, if you are a service business that visits residences, would be:

• Offering to change a smoke detector battery that is beeping.

• Bringing trash and recyclable cans from the curb to the house.

But what happens if you perform one of these extra complementary services and the customer is not at home when you visit? Have you exceeded the customer's expectations then? Actually, no. Unless the customer is aware that you have done the good deed, it will go unrecognized. And delivering an unrecognized desired service does nothing to engender customer loyalty because the customer never knew what you did.

Delivering Desired Service Tips

Always inform the customer of the complimentary task that you performed. If they are not home, leave a note: "Sorry you were not home today when I performed your exterior service. I took the liberty of bringing your trash cans from the curb and placed them next to your house."

To encourage consistency in this extraordinary service delivery program, companies should require service personnel to document these acts of kindness — and also put into place a reward system that recognizes outstanding service.

The company could run a contest and give the employee with the greatest number of documented desired services during the month a cash bonus, or possibly a weekend for two at a local hotel.

If you operate a retail business, an example of exceeding expectations would be to offer to carry the packages to the vehicle for your senior citizen customers or anyone else needing assistance.

After I take my car in for service, a day or so later I receive a call from the dealership thanking me for my patronage and asking whether I was satisfied with the service performed. Many times, I receive a follow-up questionnaire as well.

After purchasing a new laptop from Dell, I called with some questions about some installation problems I was having. No sooner did I finish my conversation than I received an e-mail thanking me for my call and providing me with an inquiry number and contact information should I need to call back. Additionally, a few days later, I received an e-mail requesting my participation in a quality assurance survey regarding my call.

Progressive, customer service-focused organizations put into place service-driven strategies that monitor their delivery systems, such as:

• Constantly look for opportunities to deliver superior customer service and exceed expectations.

• Closely monitor the service-delivery system with callbacks and questionnaires.

• Recognize and reward employees for delivering exceptional customer service.

When you consistently operate at the desired level of service, you are banking goodwill chips for any future potential service or product miscues.

2) The Adequate Level of Service

The adequate level of service is that level of service that is expected and demanded by the customer. It means delivering to them the product and/or service that they anticipate. If they purchase the product and it's in the condition that was expected and operates the way it was supposed to, you are operating at the adequate service level.

If you have a service business and the serviceperson arrived on time, did his job

correctly, communicated with the customer appropriately and looked and acted professionally, this would be an example of operating at the adequate level of service.

Operating at the adequate level of service translates to operating at the status quo. You are OK so long as you continue to deliver at your current level. However, should a serious misstep occur in your production or delivery system, your heretofore satisfied customer may just jump ship before you have had a chance to begin bailing out the water. Customer loyalty is conditional on your last successful performance at this operational level.

3) The Inadequate Level of Service

This service level needs almost no explanation. It simply means that you are not doing your job and are performing below customer expectations. Some reasons for delivering service at this level include serious quality control issues, personnel problems, on-time delivery issues and/or customer communication issues. Customer cancellations occur rapidly and in large numbers at this level, and recovery is difficult. Operating at this level for an extended period of time will put a company on the path to insolvency.

To find at what level of customer service your staff feels that you are operating, I suggest that you gather them in a room and take a poll. Begin by handing them a small blank piece of paper. Tell them that you intend on taking a poll to determine customer satisfaction levels as viewed through the eyes of your employees. Then tell them that you will be asking them to write down just one word after you finish

your explanation, and that their response will be anonymous.

Then pose the following question: At what level of service do you feel our company is delivering customer service?

Inadequate, which means that we are delivering below expectations and our customers are for the most part unhappy.

Adequate, which means that we are performing up to expectations and giving our customers what they expect.

Desired, or we are exceeding our customers' expectations.

Once the poll is finished, collect the pieces of paper and tabulate and post the responses.

Now the discussion begins. This exercise will most probably demonstrate that if you are like most companies, your employees can't distinguish between what is expected and what is desired.

Use this meeting to define the differences between ordinary products and services and extraordinary products and services.

According to my research, if we were to take a snapshot of all companies in the United States that provide goods or services, most companies operate with 20 percent of their customer base residing at the desired service level. Between 70 percent and 75 percent of their customers are receiving adequate service, while the remaining 5 percent to 10 percent perceive that they are receiving inadequate service.

It is fairly easy to measure inadequate service levels in service-based companies.

It's done by monitoring customer cancellations. All service-based companies should pay close attention to the barometers in their respective industries. When cancellation numbers increase above acceptable industry standards, it is time for concern and action.

As you move customers from the lower two levels (adequate and inadequate) to the Desired Service Level, cancellations decrease dramatically, service/product renewals increase, and product and brand loyalty increase — and so do revenue and profits.

Customers who reside in the upper 20 percent of the three-pronged group are loyal customers. They provide recurring revenue and profits through purchases of new and add-on services and products. They also provide referrals and continue doing business with the product or service provider for extended periods. Customers who remain in the Top 20 percent of the service model are also extremely unlikely to be lured to competitors for price. In fact, their loyalty means that the existing company can charge up to 20 percent over its competitors (for the same service or product) without fear of the customer switching companies, service providers, products or brands.

Maintaining Loyalty is Multi-Dimensional

Building the lifetime value of the customer is essential to growing your business. If you are to operate and provide service at the highest level, you must have a thorough understanding of the five dimensions of the customer service process.

Service Process-Based

There are four elements that represent the **service process** as viewed through the eyes of the customer each day. These are the areas in which you can make an indelible impact on your customer or perspective clients.

Tangibles

This category includes what is physically noticed by the customer, such as your advertising, uniforms, vehicles, storefront or warehouse and interior, invoices, stationary, envelopes, business cards, brochures, newsletters, Web site, etc.

Assurance

The degree of trust that you convey to your customer. Do you do what you promise?

Empathy

When a customer calls with an issue or problem, do you listen, understand and try to be reassuring?

Responsiveness

Do you respond to service requests, product orders and complaints promptly?

How well you respond during the service process will result in how likely it will be that the customer will initiate or continue doing business with you. The service process is a living process and is the collective result of the customer-to-company contact experience. If the consumer perceives you to be delivering superior service during the process, he will either:

1) Initiate business with you, or

2) Continue doing business with you.

This now brings us to the end result of the service process: the decision by the

Staying on Top of Customer Loyalty

Loyal — You have exceeded customer expectations. They are apostles. They will spread the word and give you referrals. They will pay premium prices and purchase add-on services. They are at the desired service level. They will of course renew their service agreements and continue to purchase your products.

Happy — These customers are very satisfied. They will probably refer a few customers and tell some people about you. They will most likely renew services and continue to purchase products. They will most likely buy add-on services.

Satisfied — These customers may or may not renew, repurchase, refer or buy add-on services.

Indifferent — These customers will switch for a lower price. They probably won't give any referrals if asked, or renew or give any referrals. There is no loyalty.

Unhappy — These customers won't renew, refer or buy add-on services. They will, however, spread the word about their dissatisfaction with your company.

Angry — These customers will terminate service midstream. They will most likely never buy from you again. They will tell anyone who will listen about how disreputable you are.

customer as to whether you are reliable or unreliable.

Service Outcome-Based Reliability

Reliability is outcome-based, which means that it's the result of all of the customer's service process experiences. It is when a potential or existing customer has come to the conclusion that they will:

1) Do business with you,

2) Continue doing business with you (renew),

3) Decide not to make an initial pur-

chase from you, or

4) Discontinue doing business with you.

This judgment-based decision, if negative, is extremely difficult to reverse.

As we move forward on our journey to construct a meaningful marketing program, another piece of the puzzle has been put into place: the necessity of incorporating a sustainable, quality-monitored, desired service-delivery system. Once the system is operational, it should be used as a tactical marketing advantage.

After all, Nordstrom did it. Why can't your company?

Staying On Top Of Customer Loyalty

On page 19, you will find another illustration of how customer satisfaction levels relate to customer loyalty. Simply stated, the more satisfied the customer, the more loyalty they will demonstrate. The more loyal the customer, the longer the customer's life cycle will be with your company. The longer the life cycle, the greater the revenue and profitability.

In addition, the happier customers are with your company, the more referrals they will give you, and the more add-on services and products they will purchase. On the other hand, you want to do everything possible to contain any unhappy customers — and to bring them back into the fold.

The unhappy customer tells 11 other people about his experience. Each of those 11 tells another five. That means that you could theoretically have lost 66 potential customers as the result of a misstep with one customer.

Some Interesting Facts

Only **1 in 20** unhappy customers ever complain.

65% of cancellations occur because of feelings of indifference

chapter 3
Caring for Your Employees

You may be wondering why I am including a chapter about employees in a marketing book. The reason is that employees are your greatest asset. Without a dedicated, happy team, it's impossible to deliver superior service and products to your customers. Hence, if you cannot deliver superior service and products, you cannot use them as a tactical marketing advantage.

If you try to just deliver the marketing fluff with no substance behind your advertising, you are bound to get an initial push from your campaign, but will be unsuccessful in sustaining customer loyalty.

Without a dependable, trusted, devoted and focused work force, customer loyalty can never be achieved. Therefore, new sales never reach their potential; customer retention becomes problematic; referrals are few and far between; and the pyramiding of additional product and service sales never realizes their potential.

As you may recall in the previous chapter, Colleen Barrett of Southwest Airlines noted that her employees trumped her customers in terms of importance to the health of the company. I concur with her 100 percent. If your employees don't believe in the value of your product or service, your customers never will. To be successful, you need to market to your employees first, even before your customers. Employee buy-in equals customer buy-in.

A few years ago, while in Las Vegas, I had the opportunity to sit down for breakfast with Steve Wynn. Wynn is a renowned real estate developer, hotel and casino entrepreneur, art impresario and entertainment mogul. His estimated wealth is more than $1 billion.

He was responsible for the success of the following properties in Vegas: The Golden Nugget (also in Atlantic City, N.J.), The Frontier Hotel & Casino, The Mirage, Bellagio, Treasure Island and the Wynn Las Vegas.

During our breakfast meeting, I discovered that he lived in my hometown for a short time while he attended the University of Pennsylvania.

I asked Wynn to what he attributed his phenomenal success. His response was great relationships. He noted the value that he placed on his key personnel and stated that he believed that he was the fortunate recipient of their collective devotion and hard work. He beamed when he spoke of how well he compensated and rewarded them. Wynn also made it a point to say that he would never have achieved the level of great success he had without his key people. He went on to tell me that many of the people who worked for him when he began his career were still by his side today. He also made it clear that you get what you pay for.

In order to have happy employees, you need to assess the following areas in your business:

1. Examine your salary and/or commission structure. Are you paying your employees at or above what other companies in your market area are offering? If not, it is not a matter of "if" the employee will leave, but rather "when" the employee will leave. You need to know what the competition is paying. If you close your eyes and choose to ignore this fact, good employees will exit, once trained, for the first better offer.

2. Take a good hard look at your benefits program. Today, more and more

companies are offering comprehensive benefit packages, which include medical coverage, liberal sick pay, holiday and vacation packages and retirement programs.

3. Consider offering a revenue-sharing incentive program for key employees/ managers. This program should be based upon the company setting lofty, but achievable goals within different areas of the business. Let us say, for example, that a branch office did $1 million in general revenue this year. You might then set a goal of 10 percent as the anticipated increase in revenue for next year. This means projected sales of $1.1 million, or an increase of $100,000. If this goal is met, the branch manager could earn a bonus of 2 percent of the increase of $100,000 (or anything exceeding that amount). This will amount to additional compensation of $2,000. You could also structure a similar program that allows for incremental sharing of the bonus by all members of the department (of course, clear guidelines and conditions must be set for employees who are eligible to participate in the revenue-sharing program). By offering incentive programs such as these, you are offering your employees a piece of the pie. This is a reward system based upon performance incentives.

Sharing in the company's success when times are good and goals are met can go a long way in boosting employee morale. When revenue-sharing programs such as the one described above are in place, loyal, committed and driven employees are the end result. In actuality, the true end result is happy, satisfied, long-term customers.

I am certain that some of you are shaking your heads and saying to yourselves that your company can't afford to offer revenue-sharing programs. Why should you give the store away? My answer to that is — so your store can become a supermarket.

Incentives, properly structured, can yield huge dividends. Think small, stay small. Think big, and — well you get the gist.

4. Offer a structured bonus program for add-on sales and referrals. Remember, every employee in your company is a potential salesperson. Financial incentives and rewards for employees are pathways to enhanced revenue for the company. Holding contests for the most sales in a category for the month is another way of rewarding employees.

5. Hold regularly scheduled meetings so employees can discuss or vent their concerns and/or grievances. Providing this forum allows management to get a "heads-up" on troublesome issues before they turn into major problems.

6. Provide all employees with a written job description. The job description should include a comprehensive list of what is expected from the employee. It should contain job responsibilities as well as performance requirements. Clarifying position criteria and expectations as part of the screening process prior to hiring can have a significant effect on preventing turnover.

7. Do an annual job assessment on every employee. At least once a year, management should have a face-to-face meeting with each employee and provide that individual with a candid job performance critique. At that time, you can offer kudos and/or constructive criticism. Employees value this input.

8. Express your appreciation. All employees want to feel valued, respected and appreciated. Whenever possible, be certain to go out of your way to compliment an employee for a job well done. Feeling unappreciated is a major reason why individuals change jobs.

9. Do a personality screening profile on all new hires. These tests are widely available — and for the most part inexpensive. They will allow you to assess the applicant's personality traits and determine whether they are compatible with the job position requirements.

10. Provide a working atmosphere that encourages input, openness, opportunity and teamwork. It has been

from the frying pan into the fire. Sure, most provide satisfactory initial training, but few companies provide comprehensive ongoing customer service training. These training sessions should be followed by verifiable testing to assure quality control.

The chart below lists the operational and management styles of two types of companies. Company A has a high turnover rate; Company B has a low turnover rate. With which one of these groups does your company share the most characteristics?

Before you market your company to your customers, I recommend that you market your company to your employees.

Company A		Company B
Dissatisfied employees		**Satisfied employees**
High employee turnover rate		**Low employee turnover rate**
Reactive	vs.	Proactive
Involvement	vs.	Commitment
Efficient (doing things right)	vs.	Effective (doing the right things)
Internal competition	vs.	External competition
Unilateral decisions (by owners/managers)	vs.	Team consensus
Controlling behavior	vs.	Creative opportunities
Planned technical training	vs.	Diverse training
Work together only	vs.	Work and celebrate together

my experience that companies with low employee turnover rates share an organizational mentality that encourages and promotes an "all for one, one for all" philosophy.

11. Provide ongoing training and mentoring programs for employees. This is one of the weakest areas of all. Many companies tend to throw their employees

Happy employees = happy customers. Satisfied employees yield higher rates of productivity, revenue and profit.

Don't be penny wise and dollar foolish. Look at the bigger picture. Reward your employees, encourage and support them, value their input and provide upward mobility for them. Treat your employees the way you would like to be treated if you were in their shoes. Trust me, your revenue and profits will increase accordingly.

The two diagrams below represent two different corporate organizational structures.

Chart No. 1 represents the standard corporate hierarchical configuration, which operates from the top down. This is an authoritative system and is driven by command rather than teamwork.

Chart No. 2 represents the corporate structure of a service-driven, customer-centered and employee-focused organization. It's empowered by a sense of teamwork and trust. It operates on the premise that if the customers are happy and the employees feel valued, only then will the company achieve its goals.

chapter 4
Understanding Marketing

To put together a comprehensive marketing program or plan for your company, it's important to understand how all of the elements fit together. Whether you are a sole proprietor, a mom-and-pop operation or part of a larger company, a service provider, a manufacturer, a wholesaler or a retailer, all of the same basic principles of marketing apply.

The problem is, in my experience, most individuals and companies put together their marketing programs by the seat of their pants without any knowledge or understanding of the fundamentals.

The more you know, the more information you have at your disposal. The more planning you do, the more likely it is that you will be able to take control of your marketing program — rather than have it control you.

I thought that it might be good to begin this chapter with a few standard definitions of marketing:

1. "Marketing is the process of planning and executing the concept of pricing, promotion and distribution of ideas, goods, services, organizations and events to create and maintain relationships that will satisfy individual and organizational objectives." — *Contemporary Marketing Wired* (1998) by Boone and Kurtz. Dryden Press

2. "Marketing is the activity, set of institutions, and processes for creating, communicating, delivering and exchanging offerings that have value for customers, clients, partners and society at large." — American Marketing Association

In my opinion, marketing touches, in one way or another, every facet of your business — from your invoices to your calendar giveaways, from your outdoor signage to your vehicles and uniforms, from your business cards to your brochures, from your training presentations to your employee manuals, from the way you present yourself (your image) to the way you advertise (that's an easy one), from your interactions with your staff to your communication with your suppliers. Almost everything you do in your day-to-day business operation involves and incorporates marketing, if it involves human contact in any way.

The Basics

Marketing is comprised of four basic areas, commonly referred to as **The Marketing Mix** or the **Four Ps of Marketing** (see Chart No. 1 below).

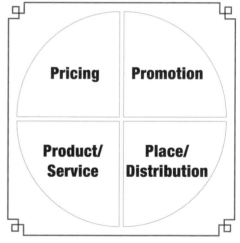

The marketing mix is utilized as part of a strategic and operational plan by the company to target and appeal to a specific market or markets. However, as I explained previously, the concept of marketing in its totality is much broader than just the above four elements. It must also include the service-sided venue of the equation that includes the existing customer base.

Therefore, I am proposing that an additional Three Rs be added to the above chart to complete the entire marketing picture. The three Rs are related to building lifetime customer value: Retention, Related Sales and Referrals (see Chart No. 2 below).

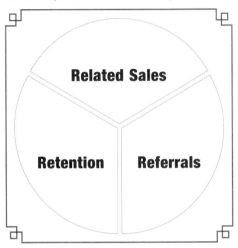

Therefore, Chart No. 1 combined with Chart No. 2 gives you a total marketing program combining the strategic and operational focus of the entire marketing concept (see Chart No. 3 below).

It's now time to define the various aspects of the seven segments that make up our new combined strategic and operational, relationship-based marketing mix. Understanding how the pieces interrelate to the big picture will make you a stronger marketer.

Product/Service: The product/service aspect of marketing deals with the specifications of the actual goods or services offered and how they relate to the customers needs and wants. The scope of a product generally includes supporting elements such as warranties, guarantees and support. Needless to say, the company and its employees must be masters of their products or services. A thorough understanding of the products and/or services offered — as well as the supporting elements (guarantees) — is essential to the success of the marketing offer.

Pricing: This refers to the process of setting a price for a product or service. It includes taking into consideration all of the product, service and labor costs involved, as well as the competitive forces and market conditions.

Every business has its own way of setting its prices. For the most part, price offerings are made based upon costs and desired profit margins. However, this may fluctuate because of other outside factors and influences. For instance, as part of a marketing campaign, the company may decide to offer a product or service at a greatly reduced price, at or below cost or even for free. This is done as part of a marketing tactic called "offering a loss leader." The object of this strategy is to have the customer purchase more than just the original advertised item, but additional profitable items as well.

Strategic pricing and loss leaders can be effective marketing tools. When developing a pricing strategy for marketing purposes, it is important to look at the big picture. Consider using loss leaders only when it's clear that the lost profit can be countered by the sales of other products or services. You may lose money in the short term, but in the long run you will reap more benefits than your initial investment.

When to Use Loss Leaders in the Retail Industry: Use loss leaders when trying to move out overstocked or seasonal merchandise or items that have become stale or are not turning over.

Loss Leader Example from the Service Sector: I have heard many smaller service companies complain that their competitors have been cutting prices and offering services at rates that seem impossible for them to go up against. They wonder how these competitors can do this, make a profit, stay in business and even continue to grow. Quite simply put, it is through the use of the loss leader concept.

A while back, I decided to check out one of these stories and discovered how one multimillion-dollar service company was effectively using the loss leader concept to bolster its customer counts, revenues and profitability.

The owners of a small pest control company came to me and claimed that they could not compete with one of the large national companies on price. They said that they were consistently losing potential accounts because of the other company's sales tactics and pricing strategy.

One day, not too long after that conversation, I sat down with an executive from that large national company and questioned him about his firm's strategic marketing and price positioning. What I discovered might amaze you. It didn't surprise me.

The national company, which I will refer to as Company X, was willing to permit its sales personnel to almost give away its residential general pest control services, at or near cost at the end of each month. This was meant to encourage the sales staff to meet or exceed their quota, with the ultimate objective of having the company increase its customer base. The philosophy was that eventually that loss leader customer will have an issue with wood-destroying insects and will need service for that additional problem.

But that initial service was not what Company X had based its strategic marketing and pricing strategy on. It was the fact that once that account was serviced, it would go under a renewal contract — and the recurring revenue from "indefinite" annual renewals would provide profitable, passive income for years to come.

The lesson to be learned here is that it does not matter what you charge for a particular service or product, or even if you are making money on those individual service or products. The bottom line is your collective profitability at the end of the day.

Many software and hardware providers market and sell their initial wares at or below cost. Why? They make huge profits with their supplementary support items. Understand the marketing mix and how it works, and you are on your way to developing an effective and successful marketing campaign.

Promotion: This includes advertising, sales promotion, publicity and selling, and refers to the various methods of promoting the product, brand or company. This is definitely the easiest of all the marketing mix components to understand. Most individuals, never having been introduced to the concept of the marketing mix, believe that promotion is its exclusive component. Now you know better.

The representation of your company through promotion vehicles is your window to the outside world. It allows you a venue to sell your wares and services and build your customer base. But too many companies view promotion as an afterthought.

Have you personally ever waited until that advertising salesperson came calling before giving any thought to what you were going to do?

Have you ever tried designing your own ad to save a few bucks, rather than hire a professional? I always found it curious that a company would spend thousands of dollars on directory advertising, but wouldn't invest a few hundred dollars to have its product, service or business marketed by a professional graphic designer.

Do you plan your yearly marketing and advertising budget, press releases and projects that you will use to generate interest in your business in advance? This is a critical component of promotion: Preparing for what you want to do. What services, projects or products are you going to feature? At what time of the year? Will you be offering incentives, guarantees and loss leaders? Do you need support materials like brochures or sales incentives (giveaways)? These are just some of the components that make up the promotion aspect of the marketing mix.

Placement refers to how the product gets to the customer — point of sale placement or retailing, for example. This fourth P has also sometimes been called Place, referring to the channel by which a product or services is sold (such as online vs. retail), which geographic region or industry, to which segment (young adults, families, business people), etc.

In its simplest form, the placement/ distribution component of the marketing mix is a set of factors responsible for all of the activities used to move a product or service from point of origin to consumption. This is probably the most difficult of all the original four components of the marketing mix to gain a clear understanding of because it encompasses a number of diverse areas under one umbrella.

In my wide-eyed view of the placement/distribution component within the mix, I can explain this piece of the equation by having you ask yourself the following questions:

• Where will I place my product/service for sale?

• What geographic areas will I service?

• What is the demographic, psychographic and socio-economic breakdown of those areas?

• What venues will I use to place my advertising?

• How will I get my products or services to the marketplace?

Retention: This refers to renewal rates and customer return rates after the initial service period or purchase is consummated. The greater the retention/return rate, the greater the profitability. This is a tangible way to measure

customer loyalty — through repeat business. Companies that have high retention rates are successful at marketing and delivering the value proposition to their customer bases. All product- and service-based business should be focused on this area once the initial sale is consummated. It is the foundation upon which ongoing profitability rests, and allows the pyramiding of sales through the offerings of add-on services and product purchases. It also sets the stage for the acquisition of referrals.

Related Sales: These are add-on sales of services and/or products in addition to the initial product or service purchased or contracted for. These sales provide opportunities for increased revenue and profitability. All companies should be focused on building this segment once the initial sale is concluded.

In the retail or product-based industries, a sales transaction may culminate in the following way: "Now that you have made your selection, I would like to show you something else I am sure you would be interested in."

In a service-based industry, the conversation may go something like this: "I'd like to share with you some of our other services that I feel you would benefit from."

Referrals: Delighted customers are happy to provide referrals. The strategic development of this resource is an important part of the marketing mix. Many service-based businesses were built on the backs of word-of-mouth advertising.

In Chapter 1, I referred to the success of Scott Cook's Intuit and its two original products, Quicken and QuickBooks. Cook built his original marketing strategy around his customers and their willingness to spread the word about the products'

effectiveness and value. Consequently, customers became "apostles" and spread the good word about the software throughout the country.

The Service/Profit Relationship*

As you understand by now, there are many factors that go into constructing a cohesive marketing program and plan. Providing superior products or technical expertise is not in and of itself enough to guarantee success. It is the people factor that is the ultimate conveyer of value. Look at the relationships among employee loyalty, customer loyalty, productivity and profitability. These bonds will define how you will conduct and market your business from this point forward.

• Internal quality represents the feeling that the employees have toward the ownership and with each other. If there is a feeling of mutual respect, admiration and the adherence and dedication to a set of core values, feelings of inclusiveness, team and commonality of goals and objectives will prevail. Internal quality yields employee satisfaction.

• Employee satisfaction levels are central to the profitability of any business. When you have employees that are compensated well, rewarded adequately, recognized for their contributions, able to achieve upward mobility, valued for their input and generally feel valued, you have employees that are loyal. Employee satisfaction yields employee loyalty.

• Employee loyalty occurs when they take ownership of their positions and responsibilities. They view company success as their success and vice versa. They may not have an actual piece of the business, but function as if they do. Employee loyalty yields employee productivity.

• Employee productivity stems from

loyalty. It is one way employees can project their feelings of delight and appreciation. They view the workplace as a venue to achieve. Here productivity is not viewed in a myopic way, but is extended to include the delivery of outstanding service and products. Employee productivity yields value.

• When employees are operating at a productivity level as described above, the end result for the consumer is the delivery of a value perception. Customers perceive that they are getting what they are paying for; hence they are satisfied. Value yields customer satisfaction.

• Satisfied customers are happy customers. Happy customers are one step away from loyal customers. If the product or serviceperson exceeds expectations, the customer will become loyal. Customer satisfaction yields customer loyalty.

• Loyal customers return to purchase more products, renew at the end contract periods, buy add-on products and services and provide customer referrals. Customer loyalty yields profitability and growth.

• Profitability and growth is the direct result of the positive interaction between each of the individual components, referred to as The Service/Profit Relationship. (See chart below.)

Leadership, although not a formal part of the service/profit relationship, is the foundation upon which the entire equation rests. It is ultimately responsible for producing and supporting internal quality. Strong leadership is the lynchpin of any effective organization. It cannot be defined in a line or in the body of a paragraph. Rather, it is the result of one's ability to inspire and motivate. A strong leader will communicate and execute the mission, vision and values of the company to his team.

Now that I have examined the foundational, historical and theoretical aspects of marketing and how they relate to one another, it is time to move on to the operational side of the equation. In the following chapters, I will discuss the hands-on practical side of marketing.

Internal Quality

Employee Satisfaction

Profitability & Growth

Employee Loyalty

The Service to Profit relationship

Customer Loyalty

Productivity

Satisfaction

Value

chapter 5
Budgeting

We write with advertised pens, drive in advertised cars, wear advertised clothing and eat advertised foods. However, many companies, particularly smaller ones, view advertising and marketing as necessary evils — a bottomless pit draining precious dollars from the bottom line.

Others don't discover advertising and marketing's true value and power until it's too late, when they're finally forced to advertise their business for sale.

Advertising and marketing are as important to a business' health and growth as fertilizer is to a crop. Without the nourishment and replenishment of new accounts, and the sustenance of current customers, not only would financial growth be severely thwarted, but the customer core would decay and waste away.

As you develop an advertising/marketing program for your company, you are faced with numerous choices, some of which include how much you should budget, where you should spend your dollars and how to get the most bang for your buck.

By the end of this chapter, you should be well on your way to answering these questions and formulating a plan of your own.

Determining How Much to Budget

As far as allocating a specific percentage of revenue to advertising and marketing, there is no exact amount that applies across the board to all industries and business segments. You need to determine the benchmark within your specific industry.

There are four generalizations, however, that I can make regarding the percentage of revenue dollars that need to be allocated toward a marketing/advertising budget:

1. The smaller the company, the more you need to allot.

2. The larger the company, the less you need to allocate.

3. Unless you are a national company, never spend less than 3 percent.

4. The more you invest in advertising, the greater your growth potential (and vice versa).

When you underbudget, two things occur: first, your growth is impeded; and second, your competitors, who are being more aggressive, affect your market share.

There are three approaches to consider when developing a marketing/advertising budget:

1. The Percent of Sales Method (Looking Back)

Very conservative firms often take the previous year's sales figures as a basis for the upcoming year's advertising budget. The advantage of this method is that it's traditional and convenient — and also subject to quick review in light of sales gains or decreases. However, this method looks backward and may perpetuate last year's mistakes. This method also tends to overlook increased costs of media and production.

2. The Task Method (Looking Forward)

More progressive firms base projections on future sales. The company sets specific goals and then spends to achieve those goals. This assumes confident, responsible and imaginative management of the entire marketing plan. It also involves constant awareness of advertising themes and trends, including close monitoring of what the competition is doing.

3. The Empirical Method (Testing/Risk-taking)

This method assumes that the way to determine the optimum to spend on advertising is to actually run a series of tests at different levels of advertising. This method requires detailed planning, patience and a large budget for testing. It also requires discipline in not drawing hasty conclusions.

Most successful advertising budgets are based on the Task method. Personally, I prefer a combination of the Task and Empirical methods. Although this combination requires more risk-taking, if monitored closely the benefits (the generation of additional revenue and profits) can far outweigh the investment. The use of this combined methodology also requires a larger investment in your overall marketing /advertising budget. This is accomplished by increasing your overall allocation percentage in relation to projected revenue expectations.

Crunching the Numbers

Let's assume that we are now ready to construct our advertising/marketing budget for the upcoming year. I have put together two examples of how to put together a budget for your company. Whether you are in a service industry, manufacturing or product-based business, the same basic principles will apply — although the benchmarks may differ (according to your industry) and the revenue stream percentages may vary.

Example No. 1: General Service Sector Company in the Northeast United States

For the purpose of this example, I have constructed a model budget based upon a company that operates within a specific service sector and is servicing accounts in the northeast part of the country.

I will assume that this company generated $1 million in revenue this year (through the end of the year — depending on when you are reading this book).

After reviewing the financials, analyzing the growth trend over the past 12 months, and mapping out goals and objectives for the upcoming year, I project 20 percent growth in revenue for the upcoming year.

Based upon last year's "actual revenue" of $1 million, if we reach our goal, the company will do $1.2 million.

It's now time to analyze last year's revenue stream. (See Chart 1 below) This will be done by breaking down the revenue flow by quarters and will be the foundation for planning the marketing budget.

This northeastern service company did 15 percent of its annual business in the first quarter, 35 percent of annual revenue in the

Chart 1 **Revenue Flow By Quarter**

The first quarter's revenue was:	$150,000 @ 15 percent revenue stream
The second quarter's revenue was:	$350,000 @ 35 percent revenue stream
The third quarter's revenue was:	$350,000 @ 35 percent revenue stream
The fourth quarter's revenue was:	$150,000 @ 15 percent revenue stream

Total: $1,000,000

Chart 2 **Revenue Flow By Quarter** (20% projected growth)

The first quarter's projected revenue will be:	$180,000 @ 15 percent revenue stream
The second quarter's projected revenue will be:	$420,000 @ 35 percent revenue stream
The third quarter's projected revenue will be:	$420,000 @ 35 percent revenue stream
The fourth quarter's projected revenue will be:	$180,000 @ 15 percent revenue stream

Total: $1,200,000

second quarter, 35 percent in the third quarter and 15 percent in the fourth quarter.

We will assume that the revenue stream percentages will remain fairly constant for the upcoming year. However, we need to adjust last year's number for a projected growth rate of 20 percent. (See Chart 2 above).

When we do that, next year's quarterly revenue projections will look like this (based on constant revenue stream percentages and projected revenue of $1.2 million).

Now that we have projected next year's growth, we can now construct our marketing/advertising budget.

I have decided that I would like to be fairly aggressive with my marketing allocation for the upcoming year, so I will allot 8 percent of my projected revenue for my marketing/advertising budget. Based on $1.2 million of projected revenue for the upcoming year, that will mean a marketing/advertising budget of $96,000 (See Chart 3 below).

We now have to decide how to allocate those dollars. In case you haven't guessed it by now, the answer is by quarter. We

Chart 3 **Annual Marketing/Advertising Budget By Quarter**

Projected Revenue:	**$1,200,000**
Projected Annual Advertising/Marketing Budget:	**$96,000 (8 percent)**
First Quarter Allocation:	$14,400 (15 percent of business demand generated in first quarter)
Second Quarter Allocation:	$33,600 (35 percent of business demand generated in second quarter)
Third Quarter Allocation:	$33,600 (35 percent of business demand generated in third quarter)
Fourth Quarter Allocation:	$14,400 (15 percent of business demand generated in fourth quarter)

Total: $96,000 (100 percent)

will use the projected revenue stream in Chart 3 to determine how to distribute our 8 percent budget.

Why do I choose to do my budgeting by the analysis of the revenue stream? Because I want to put my dollars where and when there is the most demand for my product or services. By monitoring the revenue stream, I am given valuable clarity and putting my dollars to work when my return on investment, or ROI, is the greatest.

Example No 2: Pest Management, Lawn Care, Wildlife or Similar Service Sector Companies

For the purpose of ease of understanding, we will assume that these companies are also located in the northeast United States and that their revenue streams model those in

Example No. 1.

Our second sample company, after analyzing last year's revenue stream, is expected to grow 20 percent, from $1 million to $1.2 million. The quarterly breakdown is identical to that displayed in Example No. 1. We have also agreed to spend 8 percent of projected revenue on next year's advertising/marketing budget. This gives us a budget of $96,000 (same as in Example No. 1 — see Chart 4 below).

However, the company, in this example, depends heavily on directory advertising to attract new business and puts 35 percent of its yearly advertising budget into this singular medium. As a result, this becomes a fixed expense over the course of the next 12 months. Therefore, we must adjust our revenue

Chart 4 **Annual Marketing/Advertising Budget By Quarter**

Projected Revenue:	**$1,200,000**
Projected Annual Advertising/Marketing Budget:	**$96,000 (8 percent)**
Fixed Directory Costs:	$33,600 (35 percent of annual allocation paid over 12 months)
Remaining Discretionary Dollars:	$62,400 (remaining 65 percent of annual allocation)
Budget for Discretionary Dollars:	
First Quarter Allocation:	$9,360 (15 percent of business demand generated in first quarter)
Second Quarter Allocation:	$21,840 (35 percent of business demand generated in second quarter)
Third Quarter Allocation:	$21,840 (35 percent of business demand generated in third quarter)
Fourth Quarter Allocation:	$9,360 (15 percent of business demand generated in fourth quarter)
Total:	**$62,400 (65 percent)**

Chart 5

Advertising/Marketing Budget:	$96,000	
Fixed Directory Costs:	$33,600	(35 percent of annual allocation paid over 12 months)
Remaining Discretionary Dollars:	$62,400	(remaining 65 percent of annual allocation)
Budget for Discretionary Dollars:		
First Quarter Allocation:	$9,360	(15 percent of business demand generated in first quarter)
Second Quarter Allocation:	$21,840	(35 percent of business demand generated in second quarter)
Third Quarter Allocation:	$21,840	(35 percent of business demand generated in third quarter)
Fourth Quarter Allocation:	$9,360	(15 percent of business demand generated in fourth quarter)
Total:	**$62,400 (65 percent)**	

stream based budget.

The two examples of advertising/marketing budgets cited are used to illustrate the importance of preparing a budget rather than going by the seat of your pants. Don't become too fixated on the fact that the above examples don't mimic precisely your own industry sector, however, because that was not my intent. It was my intent to get you to think about putting together your own budget, using the examples above as a starting point. It is up to you to adapt your budgets to your own retail, wholesale, manufacturing or service sector industry after determining the industry benchmarks.

Allocating Advertising Dollars

Once you have committed a percentage and dollar amount to your overall advertising budget, you can then move on to allotting funds for specific projects and media within your advertising budget.

The next part of the planning process entails the distribution of those funds according to which vehicles, in your educated estimation, will produce the greatest ROI.

For the purpose of explaining budget allocation and to keep it as simple and consistent as possible, I will use the budget example above in Chart 5 as our model for the distribution of funds.

You will find that the allocations in the quarterly periods in Chart 6 (next page) are consistent with those in the above distribution sample.

If you total all of the fixed directory advertising costs in Chart 6, you will find that the annual total comes to $33,600 (35 percent) as per our plan.

Likewise, if you total all of the discretionary allocations by quarter, they mirror the distribution amounts in the chart above (per quarter) and amount to 65 percent of our annual budget ($62,400).

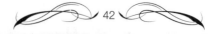

Chart 6 Quarterly Distribution of Advertising/Budget Allocation, based on $96,000 (8% of Revenue)

Fixed Costs (Directory Advertising)

Marketing Item	First Quarter	Second Quarter	Third Quarter	Fourth Quarter	Total
Directory No. 1	$4,000	$4,000	$4,000	$4,000	$16,000
Directory No. 2	$2,500	$2,500	$2,500	$2,500	$10,000
Directory No. 3	$1,300	$1,300	$1,300	$1,300	$5,200
Directory No. 4	$600	$600	$600	$600	$2,400
Cable TV		$11,500	$11,500		$23,000
Web (PPC)	$3,000	$3,000	$3,000	$3,000	$12,000
Direct Mail		$5,840			$5,840
Networking	$1,500	$1,500	$1,500	$1,500	$6,000
Community Annual Fair			$4,340		$4,340
Sales Brochures	$3,360				$3,360
Undesignated	$1,500		$1,500	$4,860	$6,360
TOTAL	**$17,760**	**$30,240**	**$30,240**	**$17,760**	**$96,000**

The entire distribution of advertising dollars comes to $96,000.

Please do not be confused by the numbers at the bottom of each quarterly column, as they include both fixed and discretionary amounts and have no actual bearing on fulfilling (or the accuracy of) our projections — other than to act as a check and balance for the overall plan.

A Closer Look at Where to Put the Money

Customers are bombarded with thousands of advertising messages each day — on billboards, radio, TV, through the mail, the Web, faxes, telephone, newspapers, magazines, novelty items, signs on passing vehicles, directories, word of mouth and all other media vehicles.

So where do you spend those precious advertising dollars? That depends upon two factors: who your existing customers are and whom you are going after. Before you commit to anything, the first order of business is to rely on historical data.

History Matters

It is important to quantify, qualify and analyze as many buying patterns and characteristics of your existing customer

43

base as possible. The more you understand about the composition of your core customer base, the more successful you will be in developing successful marketing and promotion strategies.

You need to ask yourself, "Who is the decision-maker?" The better you are at segmenting your target market, the more effective you will be at attracting those types of individuals. You can use a combination of the following to segment your market: demographics, geographics, psychographics, socio-economic groups and business/industry-specific targeting.

Demographics: What does your customer look like?

The gathering of statistical information based on age, gender, income, education, family size and other criteria.

Using demographics to target your customer: By knowing the demographic composition of your customer base and using it as a segmentation tool, you can target marketing campaigns to the decision-makers and make efficient use of your advertising placement and budget.

Geographics: Where does your customer live?

In what area do they reside? Is your base local, regional or national? Even if your customer base is national, people's purchasing habits and patterns tend to reflect local preferences for both products and services.

Using geographics to target your customer: By targeting customers by location (areas such as zip codes), you can restrict, as much as possible, your advertising placement to those mediums and vehicles that focus on the geographic

locations that have demonstrated historical usage loyalty through previous purchases.

Psychographics: What are your customer's habits?

Do you have a grasp on the lifestyle preferences of your customer base — their attitudes, beliefs, values, opinions, buying motives, product or service usage? Understanding customers in this segment gives you insight into their purchasing habits.

Using psychographics to target your customer: Imagine how targeted, effective and efficient your message could be if you were focusing on members of a church denomination, seniors group or members of a country club or environmental group.

Socio-Economic Groups: What common bonds do they share?

Is your prospective customer blue collar or white collar, empty nesters or soccer moms, members of the military or farmers? You can also target prospective customers by group characteristics.

Using socio-economic groups to target your customer: By targeting a specific group, you can tailor your message by appealing to those characteristics that the group has in common. You can use niche advertising and publications that are cost-effective and go directly to your target audiences.

Business/Industry-specific Segmentation: What business segments are you looking to attract?

If you are a business that goes after commercial accounts and sales, it is imperative that you be able to target your

niche.

Using business/industry groups to target your customer: This type of strategic market segmentation requires you to become an expert in going after vertical markets. For example, a fertilizer manufacturer would target its campaign to farmers. Some other examples of vertical markets would be advertising your products or services to industry-specific markets such as hospitality, restaurant, real estate, construction or any other targeted segment with which you wish to do business. You should advertise in industry newsletters, network within the targeted segment, advertise and link to industry Web sites, and seek out other similar venues.

Identifying Purchasing Habits

Hopefully, you have been tracking where your leads have been coming from during the past year. If you have not, you might as well be spinning a wheel of fortune or rolling the dice because you are, for the most part, operating on faith. Prudent planning and tracking reduces risk and mistakes.

Important factors to bear in mind when considering advertising include:
• Which media do your prospects use when they are looking to buy products or services?
• Which media will deliver the biggest impact for your investment?

This data can be acquired in two ways:

1. Through the use of customer surveys.

2. By maintaining accurate records of existing customers' purchasing patterns.

Customer Surveys

Solicit customer input regarding which mediums are preferred by the customer when searching for products and services.

Put together a simple written survey, with questions similar to the one below.

When you're in the market for (place your product or service here), where do you look first?

Please assign a number from 1 to 10 next to each medium, in their order of importance to you. (No. 1 indicates the greatest importance, No. 10 the least). Please use each number only once.

__ Yellow Pages
__ Local Community Directory
__ Newspapers
__ Direct Mail (home mail solicitation)
__ Magazines
__ Internet
__ Television
__ Radio
__ Personal Referral
__ Other (please list) _____

Social Media!

Of course there may be other media to choose from in addition to those listed above, depending on your market, industry, service sector or product offering. The point is to survey your customers to determine their preferences. Once you have that data, you can target your message to the precise media.

Historical Tracking

It is critical to your business that you accurately and diligently track where your leads are coming from. Most small- to mid-sized companies do not devote enough effort to this part of their business. Therefore, most advertising for these companies is placed according to the "I'll cross my fingers and hope it works" method.

Why would a business owner or executive renew an ad in a directory if he had no conclusive data to support such a move? Two simple influences:

1. The fear that if they don't renew the ad, their business might decline. Never mind that they have no idea whether that specific directory worked. In fact, as far as they know, that ad may not even be paying for itself.

2. The pressure that occurs when the advertising representative comes calling, so they go ahead and renew the ad to make the deadline.

Tracking Guidelines:

Every time a prospective customer contacts your office, a record of the call must be entered into your database — no ifs, ands, buts or excuses. In addition to the standard contact information, the prospective client should be asked the following question: How did you hear about us?

If they reply "the phone book," ask them which specific directory. Generally, prospective clients refer to the directories as a reference material after being forwarded to it by another media or source. So if they respond with "The (   ) Directory," ask them, "Was there another source you considered before going to the Directory?"

I hope that this chapter has provided a foundational look at a number of basic marketing and advertising concepts for you. It should have conclusively demonstrated that informed budgeting and knowing your customers and their buying habits are two more key elements on the path to success.

A Final Word On Budgeting

Once you get the hang of doing a quarterly budget, you can then move on to the next step: breaking down your media and dollar allocations month by month.

chapter 6
Networking

In its simplest form, networking is all about building relationships and making human connections.

Networking, used as a marketing tool, is the process by which interpersonal relationships are established and maintained for the purpose of fostering new business opportunities and sustaining existing interactions.

To build a bridge that is strong and enduring, there are two essential elements that you must invest in when erecting your networking foundation: commitment and persistence.

Building solid relationships with customers takes time to cultivate. I can't tell you how often I have heard salespeople say that they were discouraged with their results after only one or two visits to a prospective client. A solid referral list doesn't just land on your lap without your investment of time and a great deal of hard work.

Feelings of trust, reliability and source credibility must first be established before a sale or referral will be forthcoming. This requires taking a long-term approach as well as implementing short-term actions to watch your investment in "relationship marketing" come to fruition.

The concept of networking is applicable across the board — from manufacturing to retailing, from the service sector to the software industry, from product sales to the marketing of professional services.

Networking is an underused, cost-effective means used to build and maintain business contacts, and it encompasses all of the proactive steps that you take to contact and follow up with people who can help your business. The greater the number of relationships a business builds, the more it will be visible and in turn generate a large customer base to support its growth.

The general consensus among business owners and executives today is that their time is valuable and limited. They must choose from a menu of networking organizations, hoping to meet people and make connections that will increase business.

The foundation upon which the concept of networking is built is trust, and trust is the most compelling form of motivation. There is a convincing business rationale for building trusting relationships because the degree of trust that is established and maintained affects the cost quotient of the product or service.

A high degree of trust, as perceived by the customer or prospective client, can be viewed as a dividend, while a low level of trust can be a considered as a tax. When trust goes down, the time it takes to close a sale increases and the cost goes up. When the trust level goes up, the sale consummates rapidly and costs go down. Thus trust pays significant dividends. Nothing closes a sale as rapidly as the establishment of trust.

The ability to establish trust is key to every organization. When people trust you, everything else you do is enhanced. Being perceived as trustworthy by the customer goes hand-in-hand with the perception of competency. It all begins with personal credibility.

For the most part, larger companies don't appreciate the value and cost-effectiveness of building sales through the networking process. They continue to train salespeople by teaching traditional methodologies while relying

heavily on advertising to create product or service awareness.

When it comes to developing social capital through networking, small businesses do a much better job. Larger companies are slow to move away from ad budgets that focus on flamboyant campaigns with big dollars spent in traditional marketing venues.

Networking Opportunities

Joining civic groups, charitable organizations, fraternal organizations, professional networking groups and trade organizations, participating in community events, becoming active within your church or synagogue and developing relationships with non-competitive businesses within your own industry or related industries (that do not offer your product or service) allows you to promote your products or services.

Joining and participating in many of these organizations and groups also allows you to give back to the community and build good will for your business, products and services. There are almost too many diversified groups and networking opportunities to cite; however, I will mention a few at the end of this chapter. Because your time is limited, you should assess the potential ROI vs. the time involvement required.

Farming for Leads

The difference between other forms of direct marketing, such as advertising, and relationship marketing is the way you go about the process. I can relate the differences to you by using a very easy-to-understand analogy: *Direct advertising is more like fishing, while networking is more analogous to farming.*

With direct advertising, you are

presenting an inviting message to the potential customer — but there is no personal interaction, and you are looking to hook your catch with your bait (your ad). You are depending upon the message and the "impersonal" medium to attract the lead or sale. This is an example of fishing.

Networking allows you the opportunity of cultivating your potential client through the planting of multiple personal messages that will ultimately sprout into fruitful long-term and sustainable relationships. Successful marketing results from prudent farming.

Developing A Networking Strategy

1. The first thing that you need to do is to commit to incorporating a networking program into your marketing plan.

2. Next, develop a strategic networking plan. It should address areas such as:

How many employees will be involved in your formalized relationship building networking program? Remember, the more of your staff that has contact with outside resources, the more leads you can expect to generate.

How much time per week will each employee be tasked with his networking responsibilities? While it would be terrific if your employees attended these networking organizations and opportunities outside of the normal work week, you can't demand that. So be prepared to invest in this program by being willing to allocate the time and funds necessary to grow this segment of your business.

With what kinds of networking groups would you like them to be involved? *(See networking list on page 55.)*

Are there any membership fees? If so, what are they?

What are your expectations in terms of ROI from participation in these groups?

3. Hold your employees accountable and monitor the results closely. Have your employees present you with a list of the contacts they make each week, the status of those contacts and the number of leads produced and sales closed.

4. Have your employees meet regularly to exchange tips on what works and what doesn't.

5. Provide your networkers with the necessary support materials to take with them during their relationship-building functions. This may include business cards, brochures and product and service information. You may also want to provide them with inexpensive, but memorable giveaways.

6. Train your networkers in the art of referral gathering. Assuming that some of your staff who will be part of your networking force will not be professional salespeople, it's important to train them in product or service knowledge and communication skills.

Making the Most of Your Networking Opportunities

There are other things that you can do,

in addition to one-on-one networking, to increase awareness of your product or service while attending group meetings.

Offer to be a Speaker

Organizations such as service clubs and referral groups provide speaking forums during meetings. The time allotment for guest speakers can vary. But Rotary and other service clubs usually allow a 20-minute program during meetings, followed by a 10-minute question-and-answer session. Offer to make a presentation. There is a good chance that your request will be accepted.

Be sure to make your presentation interesting. I would suggest putting together a short PowerPoint show to accompany your talk. Additionally, be sure to distribute some informational handouts and business cards before you begin your presentation. Offer to hang around and answer any additional questions at the conclusion of your speech.

Display Booths

If you are offering a product or service that is used by specific trade groups or associations, consider taking booth space at their major functions. This will put you in direct contact with organizations where demand for your products and services are the highest. Your ROI is greatest in situations such as this because you are dealing directly with your target audiences.

Also consider exhibiting at fairs and consumer shows. These venues offer great opportunities to display your products and services — and to have large numbers of potential customers become familiar

with your company.

Be certain to select the correct shows for you. In larger cities, you may be bombarded with choices. Because your budget is probably limited for these types of events, you need to do your research and look into who is attending, the costs involved for display space and show preparation, how much staff you need to cover the show and what that will cost you. It's also important to find out whether any of your competitors are attending.

Booth Tips
• Make sure that your booth looks professional. In fact, if you find yourself participating in these settings fairly frequently, it is a good idea to have your booth professionally designed and constructed. Make sure that the look of the booth is compatible with your marketing identity.

• Have large graphics with not too much copy. Nothing looks worse than having a wall filled with too-small-to-read type.

• When attending these functions, you need to have enough room to display a sampling of your products and support materials.

• You should have inducements and giveaways to attract decision-makers into the display space. Consider purchasing or renting a wheel of chance and substitute giveaways where the dollar amounts are situated.

• Have literature stands that hold your promotional materials straight up.

• Consider demonstrating your product or showing a video presentation of your service on a TV monitor.

• Make sure that you are working your

booth and don't sit down.

• Don't let anyone leave your booth without filling out a customer contact card.

• Make sure that you have enough personnel to staff your booth during show times.

• Have the right personnel staffing your booth. The quality, product knowledge, professionalism and communication skills of your people matter.

• Approximately 80 percent of the people who enter your booth are not serious prospects. Qualify your leads as much as possible. Two out of every 10 of the people who enter your booth (20 percent) *are* potential sales.

Customer Contact Cards
This is the reason why you participate in these events in the first place: to increase your business database with leads. Prepare a question-and-answer sheet prior to attending the show that is relevant to your product or service.

In the chart on the next page are some examples of the type of contact points and questions to list on the sheet if you are a service provider.

Post-Show Game
Once the trade show or fair is over, time is of the essence. Be certain that the contact names are entered into your computer database and that a company representative contacts potential customers within a few days to set up follow-up appointments.

If the customer, when contacted, decides that he does not want to set up an appointment at this time, have your representative thank him and ask when it would be convenient to give him a

Sample Contact Information Sheet

Name:

Address:

Business Phone:

Home Phone:

Cell:

Fax:

E-mail:

Are you currently using this type of service?

Are you satisfied with your service provider?

Please list any type of problem that you are currently experiencing.

Please list the best day and time for our representative to contact you.

P.S. We would like to offer a complimentary inspection of your premises as our way of saying thank you for providing this information.

follow-up call. At any rate, it is important to send a thank-you letter to everyone who visited your booth.

Build Relationships with Industry Peers

I will use an example from the pest management industry to demonstrate how this could work for your business.

You are in the pest management business and a competitor performs only general pest management work and no termite work (a sub-specialty in that industry). Your company does both general pest *and* termite service. Offer to give the other company a percentage of the job, as a professional courtesy fee, if it gives you a termite referral that turns into a sale.

Approach other companies' representatives at industry functions or write them a letter soliciting their referrals, stating that you would like to have the specialty segment that they are currently not servicing referred to your company. Be certain to state in the letter that you will never go after the segments of business that you share (as that would be a breach of ethics).

Partnering with Non-competitive Industries

Once again, I will draw on the service sector to make my point. Let's say that you are providing lawn care services or wildlife control; you could then develop relationships with other service industries and work out a mutually acceptable referral program. Another example would be if you owned a home inspection company and discovered termites in a house. You could approach a pest control firm and offer to provide leads for a professional referral fee.

Remember, referral networks are a

two-way street. To get leads, you also need to give leads or referral fees. Make a point of reciprocating by sending business opportunities to those who are providing you with leads. If you find that a network "member" becomes less productive over time, replace them with a new player or company.

Religious Institutions

This networking opportunity presents tremendous potential. Approach the pastor, rabbi, priest or leader of the congregation and offer the prospect of participating in a mutually beneficial relationship. Propose that your company would be willing to tithe back a percentage of revenue for any work performed for the organization's membership. This offer is contingent upon the "indirect" promotion and support of your product or service.

The organization should be encouraged to inform their congregants of your offer through its in-house newsletter. If you are offering a service, you could also agree to provide complimentary service for the religious institution as a community service, charitable act and inducement to participate in this program.

Seminars and Workshops

Any business can have a workshop, seminar or demonstration. You can send key prospects invitations to attend, or you can visit potential companies and personally extend invitations to attend. Additionally, you don't need a lot of people to be in attendance — five or six people will do just fine. As an incentive to attend, you can offer breakfast, lunch or dinner and also promote giving away door prizes.

You can hold the workshop at your office or a local hotel or restaurant. Keep the program fairly short: Two-and-a-half hours is maximum. People don't like to take extended periods of time away from their businesses. Make sure you bring plenty of informational brochures about your products and services. You can also offer a promotional special for those in attendance that day.

However, because this is an informational session, be sure not to do any hard selling — or else word will get around that you are more interested in the sale (which you are, but they don't have to know it), than in providing the information. It's all about finesse.

Using Technology as a Networking Tool

While we understand that communication and connections are most effective with face-to-face meetings, technology has offered us additional venues beyond the meet-and-greet approach. Online activity, phone calls, direct mail and e-mail supplement our connectivity.

Tracking Results

Measuring success from referrals is not difficult. I recommend that each employee keep his own individual scorecard.

On this card, record the contact information for each referral, including the type and source of each referral, how you followed up on it, how you handled it and how you followed up with your referral source. Did you send a thank-you note, make a follow-up phone call, take the individual out to lunch? It's not hard to look back at what you did and analyze how successful you were in getting business from your referrals.

By reviewing your notes and analyzing your close ratios and what you did or did not do to achieve them, you might discover important information that will help you be a more effective networker in the future.

Developing Actionable Contact Lists

One of the primary reasons to become involved with all types of networking organizations and groups is to develop and expand your contact lists and opportunities. Each time you join another networking group, a new membership list becomes available to you. Make certain to take advantage of this valuable resource.

With these lists, your universe potential (the number of members in each organization) will increase dramatically compared to the number of individuals that actually attend the meetings.

With the list in hand, you can now call these individuals and introduce yourself as a new member — and even spend a moment or two speaking about your service or product. It also wouldn't be a bad idea to try to set up a short face-to-face meeting.

Another option, if a personal meeting is not possible, is to write to the names on the membership list and introduce yourself. Let them know that you look forward to meeting them at upcoming meetings.

Networking "Must Have" Tool

When attending networking functions, you probably find yourself getting back to the office with a collection of business cards that you have collected from prospects and must enter line by line into your computer contact software. Consider purchasing the CardScan Executive (*www.cardscan.com*).

The palm-sized device makes an image of the card and then automatically strips out the information into all the correct categories (name, company, address, phone, etc.). It allows you to download all the information directly into your computer database. This product couldn't be easier to use, and it will save you loads of time.

Potential Networking Organizations

Community Organizations
Rotary
The Junior League (women only)
Lions Club
Local Chambers of Commerce ✓
Big Brothers, Big Sisters
Local Opera
Theater Groups
Community Art Alliance
Home & School Associations
Community Beautification Clubs
Diversified Boards (offer to serve)
Local Athletic Organizations
Garden Clubs
VFW Posts

Girls + Boys Club

Professional Networking Groups
BNI International ✓
LeTip International

Trade Organizations
Local Realty Boards
Restaurant Associations
Builders Trade Association
Hotel & Motel Association
Management Group Associations

Charitable Organizations
Kidney Foundation
Multiple Sclerosis Society
Special Olympics
American Cancer Society
Salvation Army
United Way ✓
Habitat for Humanity

Fraternal Organizations
Masonry/Shriners
Knights of Columbus
Knights of Pythius
Moose

Community Events
Home Shows ✓
Fairs ✓
Community Days ✓

Religious Affiliations
Churches
Synagogues
Men's and Women's Clubs

Non-competitive Businesses
Members of your own business segment who do not offer your product or service

chapter 7
Differentiating & Branding Your Company

The first thing that I want to do at the beginning of this chapter is to clearly delineate the difference between the concepts of differentiation and branding.

They are so closely intertwined with one another that they almost become indistinguishable as separate entities. I've attempted to distinguish the subtle differences below:

Differentiation is a singular point of difference or multiple points of uniqueness that separates you from your competitor(s).

Branding represents the totality of those differences, combined with the images and core values that your service, product or company projects and evokes in the minds and hearts of your customers.

Defining Uniqueness

What makes you different from your competitors? Is it the specific product or service that you offer? Perhaps you offer the best service in your locale. Does your guarantee put your competitor's to shame? Whatever it is that sets you apart from others, you need to be able to define it and communicate it to your target audiences.

The better you are at understanding and delineating the differences that make you unique, the more successful you will be at marketing your products and services and attracting new customers.

Here are four things that will assist you in developing a differentiation strategy — and help to set your company apart from the pack:

1. Define the differences: You need to take a good hard look at your company

and products. It is important to make an objective assessment and compare your services and products to your competitors. Then, go about the task of defining the differences. This is referred to as the *point of difference proposition*. It's also known as *unique selling points*, or USPs.

2. Note the differences. Next, make note of the differences between your products and services and those of your competitors and write them down on a piece of paper. You should be able to clearly state how these benefits translate into competitive advantages over the offerings of your competitors. This is referred to as the *differentiation statement*.

3. Validate the differences. Be able to back up those differences with proof, because your differentiation statement will become part of your marketing, advertising and sales strategy.

4. Market the differences. Clearly, consistently and regularly exploit those differences in every facet of your business.

So You Think You Are Special?

Are you and your employees already using and communicating your differences to a strategic tactical advantage in your marketing program?

Whenever I give seminars around the country, I always ask the participants to differentiate their companies from their competitors. For the most part they all give the same responses: We are more knowledgeable, we're more experienced, we're more trustworthy, the quality of our service or product is superior… yada, yada, yada. You get the drift. The fact is, they are all regurgitating the same pap.

Do you think that your employees would do any better? Then call a few into your office and ask them to spend 30 seconds convincing you why a customer should purchase your product or service over your competitor.

And I am not speaking about testing only sales staff, either. Every person in your company who is part of your networking team and/or is interacting with your customer base should be able to quickly and accurately describe what makes your company or product offerings superior to that of your competitors.

This exercise will prove relevant the next time anyone inquires as to why should they select your product or service over that of your competitors. You will find it particularly useful during sales calls, attending one-on-one networking functions and during speaking presentations.

Differentiation Points

I have put together a sample list of differentiating talking points, using a theoretical small service company, for you to review. Of course, you will have to create your own unique list — but you can use this as a starting point.

• We are a family-owned and -operated company.

• No other company will take care of you the way our company will.

• We have been serving your community since _____.

• You will receive the individualized, personal attention and service that you would from a small company — along with our vast resources and professional support to better serve your needs.

• We are committed to **exceeding your expectations**.

• We offer a money-back guarantee.

• Our employees are security-screened and certified.

• Our company provides the most advanced education and training in the industry for our employees at our state-of-the-art, in-house training facility.

• We are members of the following professional associations: _____ ____.

• Our company supports the local communities we serve.

• Our company is committed to impeccable and ongoing quality control and monitoring. This ensures our valued customers of service consistency.

• Our company is acknowledged and respected for its expertise, business ethics and commitment to its employees and customers.

Once you have gone through the differentiation exercise with your employees and have thoroughly reviewed the sample list of distinguishing points of uniqueness above, it is then time to take a closer look at your own company to summarize just what precise factors make you unique.

What Makes You Unique?

I will help you work through the process point by point and then some. I have selected seven points of differentiation for your consideration within your own company.

Of course in reality, there could be hundreds of differences between you and your competitors. Examining these seven areas will merely give you a starting point.

Guaranteed. Period.®

The Lands' End guarantee has always been an unconditional one. It reads: "If you're not satisfied with any item, simply return it to us at any time for an exchange or refund of its purchase price." We mean every word of it. Whatever. Whenever. Always. But to make sure this is perfectly clear, we've decided to simplify it further. Guaranteed. Period.®

I'd like to return this taxi, please. As you'd expect, over the years our guarantee has been put to the test. We've been given countless opportunities to demonstrate our commitment to customer satisfaction and our willingness to stand behind the products we sell — though none more demonstrative than the return and refund of an original London taxi.

Featured on the cover of our 1984 holiday catalog, the taxi was purchased for $19,000 by a Kansas native as a gift for her husband (an avid car collector). In 2005, her husband contacted Lands' End and expressed interest in returning the car for a full refund. Of course, we obliged — because whether your purchase includes a tote or a taxi, your satisfaction is Guaranteed. Period.®

1. Communication

Does your ability to connect with your customers and employees make you unique? Are you known and respected in your service area and community for your relationships? If so, then make that part of your differentiation marketing and brand strategy. If I were incorporating a tagline into a strong communication centered company, it might read something like: *Nobody cares for our customers like we do.*

2. Guarantee

Do you offer a guarantee that is stronger than that of your competitors? If you do, stand behind your services and products and say so. If you are using it as a smokescreen and "marketing shell," beware. Remember, companies like Nordstrom built their reputations and brands on the backs of strong guarantees. Let's take a look at another guarantee that is used as part of a specific company's customer loyalty and brand strategy:

To the left you will find a promotional ad run by Lands' End, which is perhaps best known as a marketer of traditionally styled, casual clothing (among other things), available through catalogs known for their folksy, chatty style. The company's emphasis on quality merchandise and customer service has made it a leader in the mail-order marketing field.

There are two types of guarantees for you to consider when putting together your program: specific guarantees and unconditional guarantees.

Specific guarantees promise superior product or service performance on specific attributes (such as price, delivery and precise service offerings), while unconditional guarantees promise

performance on all aspects of service.

Compensation offers may include full or partial refunds, and token awards for punitive damages.

3. Expertise

If you are in a specialty field (like wildlife control), practice a specialty service within your organization (wildlife control within a pest control company), or offer a unique product, these can be used as strong points of differentiation between you and other companies in your service sector. Don't be afraid to use them to a competitive advantage.

If you have a bonafide expert working in your midst, don't be afraid to promote and advertise his credentials if you can use them to separate your company from other companies. If one or more of your staff has advanced degrees or certifications, make it known.

If your level of expertise within your industry is recognized by a prominent and respected organization, market that recognition through the use of quality assurance seals provided by those groups. For example, the National Pest Management Association recognizes a select group of its members that adhere to an extraordinary level of industry standards set by the organization. The QualityPro seal can only be displayed by those companies that go thorough a rigorous compliance and testing program. The use of the QualityPro seal, or a similar seal from another industry, can be used as a strong differentiation point and a significant marketing advantage.

4. Service

Perhaps your service is second-to-none. It should certainly make you stand apart from the crowd. Today, mediocre customer service is still the norm throughout most service and retail sectors.

Although the marketing of great products and services attracts customers, keeping them is a different story. In this age where information is processed almost instantly and where competitors are on your heels, companies must look inside their four walls to create a lasting differentiation model that cannot be duplicated by anyone else.

Exceptional service providers don't even have to advertise this differentiation point. That's right. It is done for them through the most effective marketing tool of all: word-of-mouth advertising. Consumers have come to expect "average"

and are stunned when they receive exceptional.

If you want to be able to deliver this type of service to your customers, you need to have your employees emotionally invested in your business and dedicated to this type of service delivery system. You need to make it your goal to create this atmosphere, one employee at a time, until you are able to get bragging (and marketing) rights.

The service delivery system has many sub-headings that should be considered including the following differentiation points:

- On-time service or it's free
- 24-hour emergency service
- Same-day service
- The home of satisfied customers

All of these elements are centered around service consistency and the ability to deliver what you promise. Many companies try to lay claim to these statements through marketing venues. Few actually deliver. Thus, their credibility is negatively affected. If you can live up to and make good on any of the above claims, you certainly can use them as part of your differentiation strategy.

5. Product Innovation

Is your product unique? Is your product original? A must have?

Have you cornered the market on a product concept and design? Have you produced the next iPod, Chia Pet Plant, Clap On, Clap Off, thing-a ma-jig (better known as the Clapper) or Pet Rock?

If so, and your product delivers on its promises, then you need to market and advertise the hell out of it, because the "proof is in the pudding!"

6. Experience

Experience matters. Almost by osmosis, experience projects and influences perceptions of loyalty, knowledge and trust. Companies that are around for a significant period of time should use this as one of their points of differentiation. *Serving our community since _____* makes a strong statement.

Another differentiation point is employee longevity. Employee permanence usually translates into service consistency. It means a great deal to a customer to know that he will see the same face or can depend on the same individual. Therefore, if you have a strong record with low turnover and can use your record of employee consistency relative to service delivery system, you should use that as a differentiation point.

7. Advertising

Your advertising can act as a differentiation point all by itself. The ways in which your products and services are packaged and presented have a huge impact on how they are received. Do you stand out from the crowd? This can be done visually, verbally or with a combination of both.

First, let's look at some companies that used visual concepts to attract customers by differentiating themselves from the pack. Their marketing differentiation points became part and parcel of their brands.

Also consider the power of words in the differentiation equation. Can you identify the companies these sayings represent?

Oh yes, just two more things that come to mind about identity and differentiation. If someone said that his father just became the proud owner of a Beetle, would you know to what he was referring? Of course you would

Visual Differentiation

Truly Nolen

McDonalds

Target

Verbal Differentiation

You deserve a break today at _____.	(McDonalds)
Just do it.	(Nike)
Snap, Crackle, Pop.	(Kellogg's Rice Krispies)
I can't believe I ate the whole thing.	(Alka Seltzer)
Where's the beef?	(Wendy's)
You're in good hands with _____.	(Allstate)
Like a good neighbor, _____ is there.	(State Farm)
Don't leave home without it.	(American Express)
Promise her anything but give her _____.	(Arpege)
_____: the all-American chocolate bar.	(Hershey)
The ultimate driving machine.	(BMW)
Have it your way at _____.	(Burger King)
It's the real thing.	(Coca-Cola)

— and it wouldn't be an insect, either. If someone asked you if you could hand them a Kleenex, are you sure that the tissue in your pocket is that particular brand? That is an example of how company identity is actually integrated into product identity.

One more thing: Recently a client of mine, Doug Brock, walked into a store in his community and began to sign a charge slip with his pen. The cashier turned to him, without ever seeing him before, and said, "You must be from Brock Lawn & Pest Control." He asked, "And how did you know that?" She answered, "I recognized the color of your pen. It matches your trucks."

Now that's differentiation — and it brings me to my next topic: branding.

Branding
What Is a Brand?

A brand is the recognition and connection that forms in the hearts and minds of your customers and through

their reaction to, and experience with, your company or product, at *every* point of contact. Brands are about people, not products. Brands are about customers, not companies. Brands are about the perception of value by the customer.

Creating a Brand

Branding is not successful unless it can convert demand into profitability. When developing your brand proposition, you must view it as what kind of perception it will create in the minds of your customers — rather than what is does for you personally. How will your brand make your customers feel? Whether you are in a service industry, the software industry, retailing or manufacturing, the bottom line is: How will your brand be perceived?

Your brand is delivered through multiple channels, such as logos, packaging, brochures, vehicles, advertising, colors, copy and mission statements, among other items. Your brand should be in sync with and represent your core business strategy.

It should create and enhance feelings of trust, confidence and loyalty in your customers. Your brand is your reputation: whether it be the reputation of your company or the reputation of your product.

A successful brand taps into emotions and people's belief systems. It promotes loyalty and drives revenue and profit.

A Brand New Image

Let's say that you have worked through the process as described and decided that your current branding image does not accurately reflect your core brand philosophy. Where do you go from here? Let me tell you a short story that could change how you view your own branding philosophy from this point forward.

A Branding Story

A few years ago, I was giving a marketing seminar for the Florida Pest Management Association. The audience was comprised mostly of pest management and lawn care professionals.

During the course of my program, I made the following statement: "I am sure that no one in the audience today still has a company logo with a shotgun pointed at an insect." To my surprise, a hand went up. At first, I thought the individual was just kidding. As I walked over to him, though, I noticed that he had a business card in his hand. Lo and behold:

That was the first time that I met Doug Brock. Not too much time had elapsed since that first meeting when I received a telephone call from Doug asking me if I thought I could assist him in building his business. The rest, as they say,

is history. I went to work for Doug as his business and marketing consultant, and discovered that he had a great company that was well known and respected in Panama City, Fla. Needless to say, at the time we first met at that seminar, his branding image did not reflect the progressive, respected company that was behind that logo.

There was a great deal of thought given to where we wanted to go with the entire branding concept. A few things to note:

1. We wanted an image that was progressive and professional. The company — and industry —had come a long way from the boot-stomping exterminator image that its original logo portrayed at that time.

2. It was important to reflect the company's commitment to the environment.

3. The Brock logo needed to reflect

and integrate its core values, which placed great importance on its employees, family and extended family (its customers).

4. The company had recently integrated a lawn division.

Below, you will note the evolution of its external branding concept.

Summary

In this chapter, I have tried to clearly define and explain the differences between differentiation and branding.

Once you have a clear vision of who you are and what makes you unique, you then have the power to channel that differentiation into a brand.

Your brand is everything you are and represent. Protect it and nourish it, for it is your corporate identity.

This is an example of a Directory Ad:

Pre-Branding

Post Branding

During the course of the company's evolution, its name went on to include lawn and pest as part of its identity.

chapter 8
The Value-Price Connection

It's my opinion that the value-price connection is so critical, so powerful and so important for you to comprehend and acknowledge that I have decided to devote an entire chapter of this book to explaining this linkage.

Fact: If the customer perceives the value to be high, he will consider the price to be secondary.

Fact: If the customer perceives the value to be low, he will consider the price to be high.

Fact: The goal of a business is to deliver the value perception at the top of the spectrum, at a price that is also at that level without tipping the value-to-price perception scale to the overpriced, undervalued side. At the level where price and value meet — at the apex of the satisfaction scale — there is an equilibrium and fulfillment on both sides of the consumer and business equation.

Fact: The more faith and trust that a potential customer has in a product, service or company, the less doubt will play a role in his purchasing decision. Hence, he will be more open to the perception of value and less sensitive to focus on price.

Fact: The more the consumer doubts the veracity or performance of the company, product or service, the less trusting he will be. Hence, the more sensitive to the price.

When many businesses, and particularly salespeople, get nervous that their products or services are not moving according to their expectations, they tend to want to lower the price when they perceive price resistance.

What's notable here is that the price will always appear to be high to the customer if the value is perceived to be low. It is therefore imperative to understand the connection between value and price. When a customer says that she is looking for a low price, is that really what she means? In the overwhelming number of instances, the answer is no. What she really means to say is that she wants something that is low cost. So you think that I am just playing word games now? Then read on.

People say they want low price, but what they really want is low cost. What is the difference?

Low price is a concept that may meet the needs of some as an immediate fix and gratification, but what if that individual discovered that the low price actually was only short term — and in the near future, that "great deal" would actually cost them more? Therefore, low price should be viewed, for the most part, as a short-term fix or gratification, where a more realistic price would mean lower cost and therefore greater value.

For example, if someone buys an inexpensive chair that looks great but is not made well, she may have to take it back to the store constantly to have it repaired. The owner may or may not fix it, depending on a number of circumstances. But let's just say the store repaired it for free the first time. At that point, all the customer lost was a trip back and forth to the store.

But let's say the chair broke again. The second time, the owner decided to charge for the repair. Now the customer had to make two more trips back and forth to the store. She also had to pay for the repair. The third time the chair broke, she decided to throw it away and buy a new chair, one that was more durable and of higher quality. Oh, did I mention that the price was also higher?

This example of the customer and the chair illustrates perfectly the concept of low cost vs. low price. While the customer originally thought that she was getting a good deal at a low price, she was actually paying a higher cost than she realized initially. And generally speaking, you get what you pay for. When you buy only for low price, you actually get less value. When you spend more, you generally get more value — and your cost is less over time.

One key to being successful at value-based marketing is to be able to educate your employees and customers to the concept of value delivery and its relationship to price and cost as seen through the eyes of the consumer.

Other keys to delivering this value-based system are building strong relationships and maintaining a high degree of quality control over your products and service delivery systems. Value goes beyond price. Today, value relates to a broader picture involving the entire purchasing experience and service delivery system.

While consumers enjoy getting products and services at the lowest possible price, there is evidence that they will pay more if the experience meets with their related needs and expectations. Focusing on product and service differentiation is a great way to move prospective customers away from concentrating on low price points.

One more thing: If you are in the service sector, time is more important today than ever before.

People are home less often, period. Therefore, time has become a precious commodity and has its own intrinsic value. This will enter into the consumer's decision-making process when the value/price equation is considered.

The Price We are Willing to Pay
Value, Status & Price

Do you recognize any of the labels below? Of course you do. Do you own any of the products that that these labels represent, or know anyone else who does? Of course you do.

Why do you think that people purchase the products these labels represent? Is it because of the quality they stand for? Partly. Is it because of their reputation? Partly. Is it because of their low price? Definitely not. Yet customers continue to purchase these products year after year, and they are willing to buy these goods at the top of the price (and profit) spectrum. Why? Because they perceive that they are receiving terrific value for their investment. And they obviously are, because they have put their money into what they considered to be a valuable commodity: status, which is nearly priceless to them.

Sure, the purchasers of these wares care about quality, durability and longevity. But the underlying and driving psychological motivator behind their purchase is status. That's right — they want to be noticed, and they want you to notice them. Hence, they are not only purchasing a product or service but the status that the product or service delivers. Therefore, price becomes secondary and the status quo represents the value proposition. If you are not convinced that the status factor has intrinsic value that trumps price, let me give you another example:

My wife and I like to go to Manhattan a few times a year to take in dinner and a show. It is only 90 minutes from where we live. We usually find ourselves traipsing around Mulberry Street after dinner. There are hundreds of retail stores within a few blocks' radius. There are also hoards of street vendors hawking their goods to anyone with a few spare bucks.

Anyone who frequents this area on a regular basis knows what many of these vendors have to offer: Stashed behind their street carts or in the back rooms of their businesses is an inventory of knockoffs.

These items are replicas and forgeries, but their label, insignia, design and appearance are so close to the original that the average person would find it difficult to tell them apart from the real thing.

Why do thousands of people make purchases similar to this on the streets of New York — and at other locations throughout the country — when they know that they are getting cheap imitations of the real thing? They are purchasing the ability to create the perception of status at a significantly lower price.

This example demonstrates that people in less-affluent social groupings who cannot afford to purchase the original items because of price still perceive value in status, and are willing to pay for that faux status. They are willing to sacrifice quality and pay a higher price to give the illusion of status.

However, I want to make it perfectly clear that although they are purchasing these faux items at a fraction of the price of the originals, the businesses that are selling these knockoffs are making huge profits because the costs involved in producing these fakes are very low.

In fact, the profit margins on the copies may be greater than the margins on the originals. This is because the people who make and sell these copies know that their consumers are not interested in quality or durability, but are focused on buying illusion and status.

The need to project status crosses all socio-economic classes. Just think about our young people who are fixated on purchasing and wearing labels like Calvin Klein or Nike. Somehow, some way, they find the money to make these purchases.

It's therefore a sound conclusion that status at any level has an intrinsic value and that value commands a higher price.

The Price We are Willing to Pay - PartII
Value, Source Credibility & Price

Determining the value of something is an individual and personal decision. Each of us has our own tipping point. But there are also many commonalities we share with others when we make our purchasing decisions. One of these factors is our internal assessment of source credibility.

Perceiving something as source credible means that we interpret it and accept it to be authentic, reliable and believable. Basically, the key to credibility is trust.

During the course of our lives, we have made internal decisions about things that we trust: people, services and products. We come to these decisions based upon our own personal experiences or by our being influenced by other individuals' experiences.

Accordingly, we assign an intrinsic value to both trust and source credibility. The following organizations and products, I believe you will agree,

fall into the source credible category.

These organizations have spent years honing their images, through the development of outstanding service and products.

When a consumer sees brands that fall into the source credible classification, it immediately conjures up positive images. In their minds, they perceive

intrinsic value — just from brand association and recognition. Therefore, price becomes of secondary focus because trust and value have trumped price, thanks to source credibility.

Why do customers flock to Sears for washing machines and dryers? Source credibility. They are willing to pay more for their products because they know that Sears will stand behind them if there's a problem. The value proposition is found in the products' durability, quality and longevity. The customer is willing to pay a higher price now because she realizes that the cost will be significantly lower in the future. Hence, the product was a better investment. These assumptions are made by the customer because of the source credibility factor.

Using Sears an example of source credibility again:

Sears' customers have come to depend on their Craftsman brand tools. Craftsman is sold exclusively at Sears, and the tools are considered dependable, of outstanding quality and a good value by those who purchase them.

Why are customers willing to pay a higher price for these tools when they can go elsewhere and buy similar tools at a lower price? You guessed it: source credibility. People are willing to pay a premium for trust.

Why do most shoppers automatically reach for the Clorox jug when shopping for bleach in the supermarket? They could just as easily choose the non-brand for less. Both products contain the same ingredients. The answer is source credibility. People trust the

Clorox brand.

Now, don't get me wrong: There are individuals who will shop just for price, looking for the least-expensive item each time. And that's OK; there is a market for that customer as well. But is that the market you're looking to attract?

If so, you'd better be willing to sacrifice individual profits on products or services for high-volume, low-profit margins — and that is a topic for another book.

The final company that I would like to refer regarding perceptions of source credibility is Toyota. I am sure that just mentioning the name is enough to conjure up images of quality, dependability and trustworthiness. This is another example of source credibility translating into value. I am quite sure that more than a few people, when mulling over the price of purchasing a new vehicle, made their purchase (putting price below value during the internal prioritization process) because of all the images that source credibility summoned.

Summary

I have tried to demonstrate in this chapter that the buyer's valuation process is not only founded on demands for utility — but many other factors as well, not the least of which are status, source credibility, delight, supplier relations and social identity.

chapter 9
Creating & Maintaining Image

I hope you've realized by now that external marketing (the marketing and advertising that you present to the prospective consumers) and internal marketing (the marketing and advertising presented to your existing customers) are all about molding and solidifying perceptions. While I have spent some time referring to differentiation, branding, building source credibility and delivering value, I have not focused specifically on creating, maintaining and safeguarding image.

First of all, I would like to define two terms for you, as I see them, and as they relate to the business model:

Image: A picture of an object: a reflection, a tangible or visual representation, creation of an impression. I would like you to think of your image as a projector in the business sense.

Perception: An observation or discernment, a response to stimuli, the ability to conceptualize, to become aware. I would like you to think of the receptor of the image, the customer, as the individual who ultimately perceives the message or image that you are transmitting and assigns a positive or negative value to it.

What I mean to demonstrate is that although you can create and project what you believe to be as a positive image, the customer ultimately decides whether you've been successful.

Customers are observing your impressions every day. They are forming opinions about your professionalism; the way you dress, speak and communicate; your ethics, vehicles, merchandise and ser-

vice. Therefore, it is critical that you comprehend the importance of your image because your customers are evaluating you and making decisions about your character and core values based on it.

How can you determine whether your image is being perceived by your customers the way you believe you are projecting it? There are a number of ways of going about this, and I will list a few of them:

Ways to Assess Image Perception:
- Quality control surveys;
- Number of customer referrals;
- Amount of repeat business;
- Cancellation rates;
- Employee assessments; and
- Interaction with customers (feedback via phone or in person).

Successful image management can generate a number of important organizational benefits, including client satisfaction, better work relationships, group cohesiveness, more pleasant organizational climates and more fulfilling work experiences.

5 Steps on the Way to Revamping Your Image
1. Determine how others currently perceive you.
2. Identify your ideal image.
3. Conduct a cost-benefit analysis for image change.
4. Are you capable of changing your image?
5. Manage the effort you invest in the process.

| NBC Logo 1956-1962 | Current NBC Logo | Morton Salt Girl 1941 | Morton Salt Girl Today |

10 Ways to Package Your Company Image

1. Logo

I discussed logo development briefly in the branding chapter, but I would like to delve into more detail here. Your logo is a critical part of your company image. It projects your brand. It is your exterior identity. Too many smaller companies do not give enough consideration to this important piece of their strategic marketing strategy. It's important to take a good, hard look at your logo and assess its relevance to your industry, business, image, core values and vision.

Successful corporations re-evaluate and re-energize their logos from time to time. In fact, even the passing of time itself will call for a good logo evolution. Mega-giants like the National Broadcasting Corporation (NBC) and Morton Salt clearly understand that changing times call for updating and modernization.

To resist change could result in looking stagnant and less progressive, thus projecting an unintentional dull, backward and possibly inadvertent negative image.

As you will note above, these strong brands did not revolutionize their image, but rather took the conservative approach of allowing their images to evolve. This type of evolution allowed these companies to keep their original identity and value proposition.

Changing your logo is a serious matter and should not be taken lightly. If after due consideration, however, you have come to the conclusion that a logo change is in order, you should hire a professional designer to create your new look.

When is the time for a **revolutionary** redesign vs. an evolutionary redesign? It is time for a "revolution" when your current logo is not accurately projecting your strategic vision.

(Refer to Brock Lawn & Pest Control's before and after logo designs on pp. 64-65.)

Sometimes entire industries evolve and actively participate in reshaping their image, as is the case for the pest management industry.

The image of the Old World, bug-stomping exterminator is just about gone forever. This is thanks to a rock-solid movement from within the industry to professionalize, led by the National Pest Management Association and various state associations throughout the country.

Today the pest management industry rightfully and proudly projects the image of its member companies as an environmentally responsible, highly educated, well-trained conglomeration

of dedicated service professionals. The Professional Pest Management Alliance (PPMA), an industry advocate, has worked fervently to project and promote this refined image through media channels throughout the country.

And so, over the past 30 years, the pest management industry has evolved from its service providers being referred to as *exterminators*, to *pest control operators*, to *pest management professionals*, as they are referred to today. It's a true evolution of nomenclature and image.

With the industry evolution comes the need for the individual companies to evolve and remake their image as well. Companies with names and logos that end with the words *Exterminating Co.* take the chance of being viewed as regressive and not in tune with the times. Names like Bug Killer, We Kill-Em, Knock-Em-Dead and others that have similar connotations evoke the same negative images that the industry has tried, and is trying, to move away from.

Progressive companies have changed their names to include words like *pest management, solutions* and *environmental services*. You get the picture. These types of names project positive images. They evoke feelings of professionalism, education, trust and value.

A revitalized logo can do wonders with both your external and internal image. Your employees will be excited and proud that you have taken the initiative to invest in this forward-looking process and project.

When redesigning your logo, you should take into consideration the following:

• What do you hope to accomplish, and what are your goals?

• Will your logo redesign be evolutionary or revolutionary?
• Do you want to keep any aspects of your current design?
• How do you feel your customers will accept the redesign?
• Will the logo integrate well with your branding?
• Should your color scheme change or remain the same?

When choosing a designer, consider the following:

• Review their portfolio.
• If possible, try to deal with someone who is familiar with, or experienced in, designing for your industry.
• Shop around and make sure that their fees are within your budget.

Redesigning your logo is not an inexpensive process, as it means that you will have to make changes to your business cards, stationery, advertising, brochures, vehicle lettering, exterior signage, uniforms and so forth. But the investment should pay off handsomely in perceived value, revenue and profits in the years to come.

2. Slogan

Do you have a company slogan? Many companies do not. Creating a slogan compatible and supportive of your company's core message conveys a strong, fresh, easy-to-remember image that will help with brand recognition for years to come.

Look at the box on the next page. Do you think that these companies have been successful in communicating a clear core message and positive image about their products and services through the creative use of their slogans?

Slogans Can Assist in Projecting Your Image to Your Target Customer

Slogan	Company
Sharp minds, Sharp products	Sharp
He keeps going and going and going	Energizer Batteries
Easy as Dell	Dell Computer
Intel inside	Intel
Your potential. Our passion	Microsoft.
Buy it. Sell it. Love it	eBay
Raising the bar	Cingular
Is it live, or is it Memorex?	Memorex
First, for you	Royal Bank of Canada
Like a good neighbor, State Farm is there	State Farm Insurance
A diamond is forever	De Beers
Every kiss begins with Kay	Kay Jewelers
It takes a licking and keeps on ticking	Timex Corp.
Because you're worth it	L'Oreal Cosmetics
Eat fresh	Subway
There's always room for J-E-L-L-O	Jell-O
We answer to a higher authority	Hebrew National hot dogs
With a name like Smuckers, it has to be good	Smuckers
Good to the last drop	Maxwell House Coffee
It's the real thing	Coca-Cola
Breakfast of champions	Wheaties
Have it your way	Burger King
The ultimate driving machine	BMW
Our customers love us... so will you!	Lindsey Pest Services

3. Color

The effective use of color in a company's logo, product design and promotional literature can have a significant and positive influence on the image that they are trying to project to their customer. Certain businesses, like those catering to the green customer, should use "environmentally centered" colors to reinforce their eco-connection. Businesses in the pest management industry trying to promote themselves as environmentally responsible can use earth tones and green hues to project their image as being in-sync with the environment. Color helps to achieve this goal by sending a positive, subliminal message to the customer.

Whatever color combination you may ultimately choose or are currently using, it should be carried through on all company packaging, including (but not limited to) vehicles, uniforms stationery, sales materials, contracts and employee handbooks.

Consistency is of paramount importance when packaging your company. All support materials should carry the logo and theme, appropriately formatted along with your company color scheme.

Color can become part of your image and brand identity. Take UPS, the delivery company, for example. UPS is brown. That color has become part of its image and identity. See whether this slogan seems familiar: *What can Brown do for you?*

IBM is blue. Almost everyone knows

The Businessperson's Color Chart of Customer Responses

Color	Psychological Response Evoked
Green:	Feelings of health, freshness, nature, natural, serenity. Effective when targeting environmental markets. Dark greens are linked to wealth or prestige.
Yellow:	Optimism and warmth.
White:	Purity, simplicity, cleanliness. Often used with infant and health-related products.
Black:	Classic, powerful, bold, dramatic, sophistication. Works well when marketing sophisticated products.
Red:	Energetic, aggressive and bold. Can also evoke a negative response, such as danger or beware.
Blue:	Banks and financial businesses use this color often because of its message of stability inspires trust. However, it can also evoke comparisons with blue-collar workers and non-professional service sectors.
Brown:	Stability, durability.
Purple:	Royalty, sophistication.
Pink:	Light pink = romantic. Hot pink = energy, youthfulness, female target audience.
Orange:	Fun and vitality. The lighter the shade, the more appealing to the upscale market.
Peach:	Evokes positive responses from customers of the following target markets: beauty salons, health care and restaurants.

Big Blue. Its color has become part of its brand. Large companies understand that the use of color plays a critical role in forming image. Color also plays a key role in product, service and brand recall. People remember colors.

4. Cards/Stationery/Envelopes/Invoices

All support materials, including business cards, invoices, letterhead, envelopes and sales agreements, should maintain a consistent appearance. Hence, the individual parts of your marketing program will fit together to form your brand and the resultant positive image that you are striving to project. Once again, the services of a professional graphic designer should be engaged to create your overall look, including that of your business cards, letterhead and envelopes.

A few words about the design of your business cards:

Your business card plays an important role in projecting your image. Its design could determine whether it is kept and filed or discarded. Size matters, and the size (if or when folded) should be 3.5 by 2 inches. Anything larger will not fit into standard-sized wallets or business card holders.

Make certain that the card is professionally designed and on good quality, professional stock. Your card should make it crystal clear what you do, and you should make sure that your company slogan is prominently displayed.

Black-and-white business cards are boring. Make sure that your card has some color (in fact, hopefully the card will be in sync with your selected company colors), but don't have too many colors. Make certain that you don't cram too much information onto one side. Remember, a creative designer can place information on the back of the card — or even create a bi-fold. Remember to include all pertinent contact information, such as name, address, title, phone, cell phone, voicemail, fax, e-mail and Web site. Remember, your business card should be creative and represent your brand with distinction. If you allow a professional designer to create your business card, the end result will be worth your small investment.

5. Brochures

Attractive, professionally designed brochures should be part of every company's marketing arsenal. Never, and I mean *never*, go about slapping together your own brochure. Smaller businesses tend to do this to save money. However, you usually get what you pay for, and an unprofessionally constructed brochure can harm your image and your brand.

It should be your designer's primary goal to make sure your brochure is so attractive, so inviting and so engaging that the recipient will want to read it, hopefully hang on to it for reference and not think of discarding it, at least not immediately.

First of all, the brochure should be attractive and stand out. Make sure that the cover design is strong and has a quick and simple primary message. Remember, it's just like your own personal advertising billboard. If the message is too complicated, takes too long to read and process, or is not visually seductive, the potential customer will probably toss it. The point of putting so much design effort into the cover is so that people will actually open it and want to learn more about your services or products.

Of course, it's a given that graphics make the brochure more engaging. Have your designer use his creativity when using them. But content is of supreme importance as well. After all, you are trying to promote and sell your services and products.

Your messages must be clear and concise because space is limited. Good writing skills are a must. If your design person can't handle the copywriting, you may want to ask him to recommend a good copywriter. Additionally, it's a good idea for the designer and copywriter to work closely together. This will produce a cohesive message.

Of course, you should include all the relevant contact information in the brochure as well.

6. Communication

Where to begin? Hundreds of books and thousands of articles have been written about communication. The bottom line? Your company rises or falls, generates profits or losses, because of it. Good avenues of communication with employees and customers enhances image and supports growth. Companies that embrace and practice strong communication policies grow exponentially. I don't care how great your service or product is: If you can't support it with strong communication systems, your image and brand will be damaged.

Conversely, if your performance excels in this area, your image will shine and reflect the strength of your organization. Companies that understand the value of communication in the strategic business sense are constantly working to improve their internal and external communication programs. How? By seeking, encouraging, supporting and rewarding employee input.

I have chosen a few specific areas on which to concentrate:

Telephone Answering Protocol

There are a few givens here:
1. First impressions are critical.
2. People don't like being placed on hold.
3. People don't like to listen to extended periods of music or commercials about your business while they are on hold.
4. People who are placed on hold longer than 30 seconds perceive themselves to be unimportant to the company, become frustrated and form negative impressions.

Therefore, whenever practical, have a live person answer the phone. Make sure that person answering the call delivers a smile with his verbal attitude and makes a concerted effort not to place the customer on hold for more than 30 seconds.

Telephone Etiquette

This is an almost endless topic, but pay close attention to this next statement: Remember, good communication is based on 93 percent tone of voice and 7 percent words.

7. Appearance

This category takes in a lot of real estate. By definition, appearance is a projector and reflector of image. How you present your product, service, company or your employees counts. In this section, let's examine two subcategories of appearance:

Personal Appearance

What you look like matters, particularly in the business world of molding perceptions. People make assumptions about you by the way you look. When we meet a salesperson or service employee — or even a cashier — for the first time, we immediately size him up. Our minds will categorize him by the way he looks without a single word emerging from his lips. What's more, we will transfer that assumption to the company whom he represents.

We naturally assume that when an employee is well dressed and well groomed, she carries a certain professional demeanor. Hence, we form a positive image of her and her company. Conversely, when an employee appears slovenly, we automatically form a negative impression and automatically assume that she is unprofessional.

Companies and employees need to accept the fact that they are judged by the appearance of their employees. Hence the best service in the universe can be mitigated by an employee who fails to comply with company dress codes and policies relating to appearance.

Almost everyone judges on appearance: It's part of our DNA. Enforcement of dress codes matters. A service employee wearing a company embroidered shirt, nice khaki pants and sneakers or scuffed shoes doesn't cut it. Sure, you can make excuses and let it slide as an owner or manager — but in the end, it's your company image that will suffer.

You are Always Being Watched

While the exterior of your employees' appearance is crucial, it is also of great importance how they conduct themselves in the outside world. Their behavior and demeanor have direct positive or negative effects on customer perceptions.

Vehicle Appearance

Companies can get more mileage per dollar from their vehicles by using them as moving outdoor billboards. When vehicle panels are used effectively, advertising messages cut through the clutter of other

10 Telephone Etiquette Tips for the CSR

1. The caller's first impression of the company is established by the greeting. Be positive, polite and professional.

2. Identify yourself and use proper English. Do not use slang.

3. Listen to what the caller is saying.

4. Avoid interrupting the caller or being distracted during the call.

5. When placing the caller on hold, request his permission first, then wait for a response.

6. Always inform the customer prior to transferring the call.

7. Make certain to inform the individual receiving the call of the caller's name and purpose.

8. If the individual requested by the caller is not available, apologize and let her know that her call is important and that she will receive a call back as soon as possible.

9. If the customer has an issue, always empathize with him.

10. Always say "thank you for calling" before hanging up.

competing forms of marketing.

There are a few different ways to go with this type of advertising campaign. You can have the graphics painted on the vehicle. You can have vinyl letters and graphics placed on your van, car or truck. Or you can go with a partial or full vehicle wrap. I prefer the full wrap, but it is the most expensive way to go. Any of the three options you choose will require the services of a professional. A word of caution: Don't overclutter your moving billboard. Also, make certain that your phone number and Web address are easy to read.

8. Testimonials

Testimonials are a great way to market your company. They give you the credibility of a third-party endorsement. They go a long way in projecting a positive image for your company. Testimonials should become part of your company's promotional strategy regardless of what industry you're in.

Your sales staff should include a selection of testimonials with their presentations. Nothing sells products or services like satisfied customers. Additionally, you should set up a page of testimonials on your Web site.

The most effective testimonials are written on company or personal letterhead. Of course, this requires that the customer take the time and make the effort to produce this for your company. There are a number of ways that you can go about soliciting testimonials from your customers:

• Ask your customers to write a personal testimonial letter: "I would really appreciate your writing a testimonial letter for me outlining how happy you are with our product/service."

• Offer to write it for them: "I know that you are very busy and I would really appreciate your writing a testimonial letter for me, but I'd be more than happy to draft something for you to edit."

• When a customer displays satisfaction with your service or product, ask at that time: "I am thrilled that you are satisfied. Would you please write your comments down on your letterhead? I would love to use it as a testimonial."

• One easy way to collect testimonials is to include a link on your site with a form that allows your customers to give you their votes of confidence.

• Anytime you receive a great letter or e-mail from customers, ask them whether you can use their comments to recommend your products or services to others.

• When you mail out quality assurance surveys, leave a space for comments/testimonials: "If you are happy with our product or service, please describe your experience below." Beneath the comment line, you will need to make the following statement: "Do we have your permission to use your valued testimonial in our advertising or promotional literature? Please check yes or no." Of course, place two boxes next to the appropriate response.

There are some things that you can do to get the most impact from your testimonials, such as:

Make sure that each testimonial has as much identifiable information as allowable. This gives it more credibility. Testimonials attributed to "Mrs. J. from NY" are worthless.

Ask your customer to write a comparative testimonial. For instance, if she called you after having an unhappy experience with another company or product, she should state that in her testimonial: "Three other companies tried to solve my problem and couldn't, but your company did."

9. Advertising

Good advertising brings in clients and revenue, and ineffective advertising costs you money with no return on investment. A good ad portrays your company in a positive light. It uses graphics and content optimally.

The "Professional," the Truck & the Soda Can

I was driving down a highway in Tucson, Ariz., on my way to visiting a client, when I noticed a service vehicle in front of me that caught my attention. The signage was attractive and the branding was outstanding. The vehicle glistened in the desert sun. As I pulled next to the truck, I couldn't help but note the catchy slogan and attractive lettering on its side panel: "We Care for Our Environment." What a professional-looking representation of the company, I thought.

Then something unbelievable happened. As the truck sped up and edged over to the right lane to get off at the upcoming exit, I noticed a hand coming out of the driver's side window. As the truck proceeded to the exit and I continued down the highway, passing it to the left, a soda can came flying out of the driver's window onto the shoulder of the road.

I couldn't believe my eyes.

All I could think about was all the effort and money that the company had invested in branding its professional image. All of that goodwill was gone in a flash, thanks to the actions of one inconsiderate employee. The impression created by that employee would most certainly be processed by any passers-by observing this behavior, as follows:

1. The driver is a slob.
2. The driver has no respect for my community.
3. The driver has no respect for the environment.
4. The driver is unprofessional.
5. The driver is untrustworthy.

By extension:

1. I would never want to do business with this individual.
2. I would never want to conduct business with this company.
3. I cannot trust the company.
4. The company says one thing and does another.
5. The company is unprofessional.

It's imperative for companies and employees to remember that while they are servicing accounts, driving marked company vehicles (on or off duty) or wearing company apparel, that potential customers are watching and observing their appearance and demeanor. Company policies should stress the importance of maintaining a positive image at all times.

Advertising is such an important part of your marketing and business strategy that you should use professionals to create your ads. Many parts of the advertising puzzle affect image perception, including color, graphics, content, spacing and production. The perception of a good image will play a major role in moving the customer to action. I will address this topic in more detail in Chapter 17, "Advertising, The Media & The Message."

10. Web Presence

Today's customers expect to be able to find and communicate with a business online. Not having a professionally prepared Web site reflects poorly on your image. Your site should convey the consistency of image that exists throughout the rest of your company. Each page, beginning with your home page, should be considered an individual picture frame and informational depository. It must paint a picture of your vision while at the same time engage your "audience" to act.

Summary

All of the factors referred to in this chapter play an important role in the projection and perception of your image. Guard it carefully; protect it with all of your assets. Once it is tarnished, it's almost impossible to regain.

In summation, your image is the set of qualities and characteristics that represent perceptions of your competence and character as judged by your customers, employees, suppliers, business associates and the public.

chapter 10
Buying & Selling

There have been hundreds, no thousands, of books and articles written about buying and selling. Marketing by definition embodies and embraces all aspects of sales and buying patterns as it strives to determine what drives the consumer to a purchasing decision.

In this chapter, I will attempt to break down and explain the buying/selling process into its most simplistic form, thus giving you a basic understanding of what motivates customers to buy.

What Motivates People to Buy?

Obviously, people's buying decisions are motivated by a number of different internal and external stimuli and influences. About 75 percent of buying decisions are based upon subconscious needs and wants such as feelings of prestige, habits and perceived value. If we can understand what factors are behind the decision-making process, and what emotional drivers trigger the sale, we will be more successful in our marketing and selling efforts. People purchase goods and services for a number of core reasons; below you will find a few of the major ones:

• They are interested in finding solutions to their problems and want results.

• They are attracted to the benefits and/or features of a particular service or product.

• The product or service will reinforce or elevate the image they have of themselves.

• The guarantee or warranty will be the driver of the close.

• They will have a great deal of trust in the company or product.

• They will have formed relationships with someone in the company.

• They will make a purchase based on quality.

• They will base their purchase decision on convenience.

• They will base their decision on emotions.

• You may be providing a selection of products or services difficult to duplicate.

• You may be offering products or services that are unique.

• To a small segment, price is of paramount importance. They will find value in the lowest price.

Now that we understand why people purchase goods and services, let's examine what makes them actually buy: People buy because they have a need that clamors to be fulfilled and a want that needs to be met.

Some Core Needs and Wants:

• Comfort
• Communication
• Convenience
• Dependability
• Durability
• Efficiency
• Ego-fulfillment
• Increased standard of living
• Peace of mind
• Protection
• Recognition
• Safety
• Up-to-date technology

Let me give you an illustration of how the simple purchase of a shirt exemplifies what goes through the subconscious mind of a consumer prior to making a buying decision. Consider just how many of the above criteria are met as part of the choice process. I will list them after you read the cited example below:

A potential customer walks into Bloomingdale's with the purpose of purchasing a sport shirt — not just any shirt, but a Ralph Lauren Polo shirt. Any shirt at a fraction of the price would have met the utilitarian needs of the customer. However, this individual was willing to pay a premium for this particular shirt because the label provided him with status.

Analysis of the purchase of one Ralph Lauren sport shirt:

- The customer trusts the reputation of the product and the store.
- The store guarantee acts as a value-added benefit.
- The product elevates the image of the consumer and provides status.
- The product is durable.
- It is a quality product.
- The consumer is emotionally invested in the brand.
- The product meets ego-fulfillment needs.
- It gives the customer desired recognition.
- It is demonstrative of an increased standard of living.

Let's look at some other examples:

Let's say that you are making plans to go on vacation and are considering hotel accommodations. You don't realize it, but subconsciously a lot of things are going through your mind that are involved in guiding you toward your hotel selection. You are processing thoughts such as: "I want to stay at a place that will deliver comfort, contentment, peace of mind and protection." It needs to be a place that you can trust, that is attractive and that will meet your standards (ego-fulfillment).

When you consider an airline, unless you are solely price-focused, you will think about factors such as, "Will it be a direct flight?" (convenience) "Will they get me there on time?" (dependability and efficiency) "How is their safety record?" (peace of mind)

You may also consider purchasing flight insurance for your trip. You are doing this because you are taking into consideration core subconscious feelings such as protection, peace of mind, trust and emotion.

For my next example of analyzing the relevancy of core vales and customer needs and wants, and how they apply to a specific industry segment, I would like to once again look at the pest management industry.

Let's say that a potential customer notices a termite swarm and will be looking to hire a pest management company in the immediate future. What goes through this individual's conscious and subconscious mind when she is going through her initial selection process of whom to contact?

First, and foremost, she wants results. She also thinks about more encompassing issues, such as:

- "Is this a company that I can trust? (peace of mind)
- "Will they protect my home from damage?"
- "Will the materials that they apply pose any problems for me or my family?" (safety)
- "Will they look and act professional?" (image)
- "Will they stand behind their work?" (guarantee)
- "Since my husband and I work

during the week, can they do the job on the weekend?" (convenience)

• "Will the company respond quickly?" (immediate response – this consumer's "need and want" applies to a certain segment of service providers)

These examples illustrate the concept of seeing beyond the obvious simplistic reasoning for the purchase decision and delving into the psychological motivators behind the buying process. Even the most basic purchasing decisions evolve from our core reasoning process.

By understanding the "buyer/seller dance" and the needs and wants of their customers, companies can develop marketing campaigns and programs based upon certain buying patterns and assumptions relating to their target markets' demographics and characteristics.

Before I discuss how you can use this information to put together effective advertising campaigns or demonstrate how it can help your sales department close a sales call, I want to talk about some other key aspects of the buy/sell mantra.

Customers make purchases based on emotion, and find ways to rationalize their decisions based upon reasoning.
Consider all of the purchases that you have made during your lifetime, and just how many of those buying decisions were based on products or services that you just *had* to have. Also consider how many products or services that you bought based on impulse.

How many purchases have you made because you had a comfort level (strong positive feelings) dealing with a service provider, an employee or a company?

Do you recall that shirt or tie, car or vacation, health club membership or thingamajig you couldn't live without? Somehow you found a way to convince yourself (and maybe your spouse) that it was a sound purchase decision, regardless of the actual reason.

Yes, feelings and emotions drive purchasing decisions over rationality and reasoning, which brings me to my next observation when it comes to trying to influence the consumer.

Don't sell, market or advertise what you want; sell what your customer wants.

This is one of the most significant errors that many smaller companies make. Rather than market and sell based on reliable assumptions of what best meets the needs, wants, core value system and emotional triggers of its target customers, the company will forge ahead, focusing on the "features" its product or services offer. (Please refer to the previous lists that summarize core wants and needs).

Selling Benefits vs. Features

Now that I have explained what conscious and subconscious considerations go through the minds of potential customers (relating to their wants, needs and core values), it's time to discuss how the presentation of features and benefits enters into the sell/buy equation. While it is understandable that companies want to focus on the features that their products and services offer, it's even more important for them to translate those features into benefits. It is only then that the customer is able to perceive the value of their product or service. Let me first explain by defining the differences between features and benefits.

A feature is a physical attribute or element of a service or product; a benefit is something that adds value to the sales process.

Generally, when a consumer considers making a purchase of either a product or a service, it's done with a significant amount of emotional investment in the process. They have an emotional reaction to something. When you combine that with demonstrating the benefits of the product or service and matching it up with their needs, the sale closes.

An example of a product feature of a car would be a GPS system. It seems like a really neat technological advance that many people find attractive. The benefit would be that it gets you where you want to go without getting you lost, which would save you time.

Here is another example. You are considering purchasing a new vehicle that is advertised as fuel-efficient. The feature is that the car gets 40 miles per gallon. The benefit is that you will save a fortune in fuel costs.

I also want to provide you with an example of how this feature/benefit relationship works when you are selling a service. For this, I will use a landscaping company to make my point.

A landscaping company may promote an organic material to control weed growth in its ads. The targeting of the organic material would be viewed as promoting the feature. The benefit would be that the customer's lawn will look beautiful and green, and will make him proud to have his neighbors pass by his home. Another benefit would be that he is doing his part as a good environmental steward by hiring a company that applies organic materials.

Taking into consideration the feature/benefit relationship, it would be in your company's best interests to focus on promoting the benefits of using your products and services, as well as listing the features, because it's clear that people consider service initially because of their features but don't usually commit to purchasing them until they are convinced of the benefit.

Insightful companies come to the realization fairly early on that when the consumer is making his purchasing decision, he is buying much more than a particular product or service. He is also purchasing the other intangibles that go along with that product or service. Let me give you an example of what I mean.

When a woman goes to a beauty salon to get her hair cut or colored — or to take advantage of any other number of services — is the actual service the only thing that matters to her? How about the conversation that she looks forward to each visit with the people who provide those services? How about the personal feeling of satisfaction that she gets when she leaves the salon?

It should be crystal clear to you by now that customers make their purchasing decisions based on their belief systems. Therefore, as a marketer of your services and products, you should be attempting to identify and penetrate your target customers' emotional action buttons. This can be facilitated through benefit-based advertising and sales programs.

> ## The formula for success:
>
> Value = $\dfrac{\text{Benefits (Needs/Wants/Emotions)}}{\text{Price}}$

Simply put, if the benefits that you provide to the customer through meeting their needs and wants are greater than the price you are asking, then the customer will perceive value and purchase your service or product. Conversely, if the price is greater than the perceived value, then the customer will not purchase the service or product. Therefore, you have a few options to consider when marketing your services and products.

Advertising & Marketing Products & Services

So now that I have reviewed with you the secrets to affecting customer action, how do we translate that into creating effective advertising?

As I stated earlier, if you want to increase sales, you must **focus** on the benefits of your products or services, not just the features.

Your ad or brochure should explain how your product or service will help the consumer. It should address fundamental questions, such as: "If I buy this product, how will it make my life better?" "Will it make me feel better about myself?" "Will it make my life easier?" "How will it solve my problem?"

Whenever you say what your product or service does (a feature), ask yourself, "How will that feature help my customer? What is the benefit of that feature?" If you do that and explain it clearly, you will immediately see your sales increase.

I suggest that you review your product and service offerings and make a list of features and benefits that you can refer to in preparation for your advertising or promotional campaign.

Let's assume that your advertisement in the phone directory piqued the customer's attention. Your ad did a great job stressing the benefits that the customer was searching for. The ad moved your potential customer to action. Hence, your office received a phone call. The customer service representative takes down all the pertinent information and sets up an appointment for a sales representative to visit.

I want to pause here for a moment. What I hope to do during the remainder of this chapter is to take some marketing applications and apply them to the service/sales sector. Because selling is an important part of marketing, I felt that I could not ignore this subcategory of relationship marketing.

Selling Service

- To sell in today's environment, you must partner with your customers, seeing from their perspective and helping them through the buying process.
- The more time the customer takes to mull a decision, the less likelihood there is that he will buy.
- Most customers love to purchase services and products, but they find the sales process distasteful.

Back to the Basics

So the ad worked; the office person made the appointment for the sales call and now the marketing and sales responsibility of the product or service falls to the salesperson. Remember, all the lessons learned relative to customer needs and wants, core values, features and benefits still apply and extend to face-to-face sales calls. The most important thing that our salesperson needs to do is to uncover the needs of the customer (after he or she says hello and exchanges pleasantries, of course).

It is imperative that the salesperson works to build a relationship with the customer through his communication skills. That is his first responsibility. Once that goal is secured, he can then proceed. It would be to his great advantage to be perceived as an adviser rather than a product or service "hawker."

It's important for the salesperson not to forget that the customer buys when the customer trusts, feels reassured, has his needs met, appreciates the benefits and perceives value. Those things are never achieved by focusing exclusively on the technical side of selling the product or service.

Establishing an understanding of what the customer needs and wants trumps any initial discussion of features or benefits. Once you identify what the customer wants and needs, you can then move forward to discuss benefits of the products or services and offer solutions to meet their needs.

This kind of relationship-focused sales approach adds value to the buy-sell process and fortifies the way the salesperson and company are perceived by customers.

Experienced and trained sales personnel understand that the way to learn about customer needs comes through questioning. Good salespeople spend a great deal of time listening, while inexperienced or ineffective salespeople spend most of their time doing all of the talking.

Top salespeople identify the problems or needs through the eyes of the customers, and view the solutions in terms of what is best for their buyers.

Astute salespeople will help their clients evaluate product or service options and view the initial relationship as an opportunity to develop a long-term association. They will make recommendations regarding products or service options as they build trust and move customers toward purchases.

Oh yes, one other thing: If during your close, your customer makes the statement, "I just need some time to think over my decision," in most instances it means that you have not demonstrated enough value during your presentation. Remember, people buy on feelings and justify their decisions with logic. If logic enters the picture first and feelings take a back seat as the primary driver for decision-making, it's probable that you will lose the sale. You must therefore try to ascertain where you faltered in your presentation and how you can be more effective addressing and meeting the needs of customers.

It is not enough just to understand these consumer shifts in attitudes. As marketers, we must take this raw data and translate it into an actionable strategy that will assist us in selling our products and services.

Let's examine how we will use these consumer habit shifts to our advantage.

Because the customer has such unfettered access to information and research, we need to be sure that our salespeople and support staff are completely versed in product and service knowledge. It is no longer acceptable to have a general understanding of the goods and services that you offer. They must be "at least as expert" as the customer who is making the purchase.

They need to know the product and service offerings inside and out.

Understanding Today's Customers vs. Yesterday's Customers

As part of your marketing and sales program, it's important that you recognize a number key factors relating to consumer attitudes and how they have changed.

Level of Knowledge
People today are more knowledgeable than ever before. They have almost instantaneous access to innumerable reference materials and information resources.

Research Access
The Internet has opened up the world of information for the consumer. They can readily compare your service and product offerings with those of your competitors in a flash.

Demand Factor
Because of this increased knowledge and availability of information, consumers are more demanding than ever. If you cannot meet their needs, they will find someone else that can.

Trust
As years have passed, people's trust levels have declined. They have become more suspicious of businesses' ulterior motives. This lack of trust has been fueled by the media exposure of corporate greed (Enron, Tyco, et al) and the profiteering of many large conglomerates.

Physical Access
When I was a child in the 1950s and early 1960s, it was common for the father to be out working and for the mother to be at home. Obviously, that scenario is ancient history. Today people are at home much less than years ago. They are working or running around with the kids. Therefore, physical access is much more limited. Interestingly, though, people are easier to get hold of with cell phones and e-mail.

Value/Price Sensitivity
Because of the aforementioned factors — knowledge, access, demands and trust — consumers are much more concerned with receiving value for their investment.

Companies must commit significant resources to training programs to ensure that their sales force is more educated and better prepared than their competitors.

Just as we understand the importance of increasing our core products and service knowledge, so must we work to improve our ability to communicate and build interpersonal relationships with our customers.

As I explained previously in this chapter, people buy on emotion. People

trust less today, so it is crucial to the sale to build bridges of confidence with our buyers, to refocus our efforts on identifying and meeting the customer's needs.

Through the use of relationship marketing and honed communication skills, it's possible to influence the customer's belief systems in the salesperson's quest to drive them toward the purchase.

To accomplish this goal and increase our influence, however, the salesperson must be adept at sizing up his prospects and relating to them on their particular level. This is important because people buy products and services that appeal to their own visual-, auditory- or sensory-driven thought patterns.

Identifying Personality Styles During the Selling Process

There have been volumes of books, research papers and articles written on the subject of how to identify and impact consumer behavior, and it feels like I have read most of them. Almost every author of every sales book has his own opinion of what works and what doesn't.

In these books, papers and articles, there are charts, graphs and opinions that all seem plausible. However, as believable as they are, is it practical to expect the average salesperson to study and apply these theories? What personality profiles from which authors should they use? Most of the identity characteristics are pages long. Will the average salesperson ever learn them, alone master them? No.

He will read the books, find it all interesting, probably agree with most of it and then place the book on a shelf

— only to be viewed as a reference tool from time to time.

So I am giving you the benefit of my doing much of the work for you, going through reams of information and data and reducing it to what I believe is the essence of what a salesperson needs to be effective at relationship marketing.

In my opinion, if your sales staff masters these few cues, it will give them tremendous advantages in understanding their customers' personalities and allow them to interact with them on a much more intimate and compatible level. Once they get it, understand it and practice it, I guarantee that their close rates will dramatically increase. Here we go:

There are three basic personality styles in the world: visual, auditory and kinesthetic. While we all contain fragments of each style in our behavior patterns, nearly all of us have a dominant trait. It is to the great advantage of the salesperson to be able to identify the dominant personality trait and interact with the customer on that same level. If he accomplishes this, he will be more successful at establishing comfort levels with customers, as well as building up the trust quotient. Hence he will be more effective in closing sales.

The Visual Personality

Individuals with this personality type move quickly, use their hands to gesture, talk at a rapid pace and use visual cue phrases, such as: "I would like you to see this." "I understand your point but won't you please look at it my way." Some other visual key words are: view, observe and watch. Visually oriented people like to look at things. If you are a salesperson,

you should present them with pictures and brochures. Conversely, they are turned off by long-winded explanations. Visually oriented people are irritated by salespeople who move and speak slowly and methodically, so adjust your pace accordingly.

The Auditory Personality

This type of personality style moves slowly and methodically. They speak at a slow pace and use auditory cue phrases, such as: "I'm listening to you." "I hear what you're saying."

Auditory oriented people appreciate explanations. If you are a salesperson, you can take comfort in knowing that they want you to explain everything point by point. Conversely, auditory personalities do not like to look at pictures or brochures. They would prefer having the material explained to them. So do your presentation and leave the brochure with them to read later. Additionally, auditory individuals are irritated by fast-paced, quick-moving salespeople. Talk slowly and try not to fidget.

The Kinesthetic Personality

This type of individual is very easily identified. They are the touchy-feely types. You know the kind: They slap you on the back and say, "How ya doin'?" They grab your hand and shake it like a bag of chicken seasoning. They use kinesthetic cue phrases like: "I need to feel a comfort level with you." "I sense that we are on the same page." These individuals base their purchasing decisions almost entirely on their relationship perception with the salesperson.

Non-verbal Communication

In addition to being able to read personality styles, there are other basic physical clues to watch out for during the sales process. By adding these to his repertoire of customer assessment tools, your salesperson will be set to take on his role as a true customer relationship consultant.

Mouth Covered/Nose Touching

Customers who are either placing their hands over their mouth or touching the bridge of their nose during your sales presentation are giving you a subconscious clue that indicates that they do not believe what you are saying and that you are being deceptive. Therefore, when you notice these reactions, you should use them as opportunities to restate product or service value. You should also use it as an opportunity to seek more information from the customer.

Ear Touching/Ear Tugging

If the customer is fidgeting, touching or tugging at their ear, it is a subconscious clue that they are not listening to you. Perhaps you have turned them off. They may be looking at you, but they are not hearing what you're saying. Use this cue as an opportunity to refocus their attention.

Arms Folded

This is an easy one. If someone is standing there, or sitting for that matter, with their arms folded, it means that he has built a wall between the two of you. Obviously, this is not a good thing. You need to do a quick reality check and discover the

reason. It could be as simple as you failed to build a relationship before you began your pitch, or perhaps you talked a visual person to death. Maybe you insisted on showing an auditory person pictures — you get the point. But one thing is for certain. If you don't break down that wall, it's goodbye sale.

I have one final comment about interpreting non-verbal communication clues: It's possible that someone is covering his or her mouth because of a cold, a cough or bad dental work. They also could be touching their nose because of an itch or a cold. You need to use common sense when interpreting all verbal, physiological and non-verbal clues.

Sales and marketing go together like peaches and cream. They become better when they complement one another. The best marketing program to attract customers to your company or product will never reach its potential without a strong sales program and well trained sales force.

In today's competitive business world, excelling at relationship marketing could make the difference between sale or no sale.

chapter 11
Take a 'SWOT' at Your Business
(Strengths, Weaknesses, Opportunities & Threats)

Most owners of small to medium size companies are unfamiliar with the term SWOT analysis. It simply is an acronym for examining the Strengths, Weaknesses, Opportunities and Threats of your business.

Doing an analysis of this type should be part and parcel of your annual strategic planning. It's helpful every now and then to lift your head above the day-to-day grind to consider how you will deal with the future.

A SWOT analysis provides direction and serves as a basis for the development of business and marketing plans. It accomplishes this by assessing an organization's strengths (what an organization can do) and weaknesses (what an organization has been unable to do), in addition to opportunities (potential favorable circumstances for a business) and threats (potential unfavorable situations for an organization).

The point of performing a SWOT analysis is to take the information that you have learned and separate it into internal issues (strengths and weaknesses) and external issues (opportunities and threats).

Once the analysis is completed, your company will be able to take the information from the SWOT analysis and move forward with an action plan based on your findings. This document can stand on its own or be used as an addendum to your marketing plan.

A SWOT analysis will help you look closely at the following areas:
- Service and/or Products (what are you selling?)
- Process (how are you selling and marketing your products and services?)
- Customer (to whom are you selling your products and services?)
- Distribution (how are they delivered to your customers?)
- Finance (what are the prices, costs and investments involved?)
- Administration (how are you managing the process?)

Strengths & Weaknesses: An Overview

Owners and managers need to begin thinking in terms of what your company can do well and where it may have deficiencies. Strengths and weaknesses exist internally within a firm, or in key relationships between the firm and its customers. Your SWOT analysis must be customer-focused to gain the maximum benefit from this exercise.

While focusing on the internal workings of the company is critical, it's just as important not to ignore the external environment, which includes the opportunities and threats that exist outside the walls of the company from exterior forces. Companies that are caught

	Supportive	Harmful
Internal	1. Strengths	2. Weaknesses
External	3. Opportunities	4. Threats

up in developing strengths and minimizing weaknesses may ignore the external environment. A mistake of this magnitude could lead to an efficient organization that is no longer effective when changes in the external environment prohibit the firm's ability to deliver value to its targeted customers.

On the opposite pages, you will find a typical SWOT analysis chart. This will help you better understand how the concept functions as you're working through the process. This chart contains a separate quadrant for Strengths, Weaknesses, Opportunities and Threats. Your SWOT analysis should be broken down into these four separate sections:

Quadrant I: Strengths

Areas that are supportive in having you achieve your goals. Areas in which you excel. These things are internal in origin and are attributes of your organization.

What do you do well? What advantages do you have over your competition? Strengths describe the areas in which you excel, both tangibly and intangibly, within your company.

Strengths include the positive attributes of the people involved in the business, including their knowledge, backgrounds, education, credentials, contacts, reputations or the skills they bring. Strengths also include tangible assets, such as available capital, established customers, existing channels of distribution, copyrighted materials, patents, information and processing systems, and other valuable resources within the business.

Strengths capture the positive aspects internal to your business that add value or

Questions to Analyze Strengths

1. What is the company's average annual rate of growth?
2. What is the company's average annual rate of profit?
3. What are the major sources of the company's revenue and profit?
4. Does the company have a strong brand?
5. Is the marketing/advertising effective?
6. What is the major focus of the company?
7. Does the company have a pool of skilled employees?
8. Is the morale of the employees high?
9. Are there rewards in place to create an atmosphere conducive to excellence?
10. Does the company have adequate financial resources to facilitate growth?
11. Does the company harness information technology effectively?
12. Does the company manage its inventories efficiently?
13. Has the company demonstrated the ability to adapt and change?
14. Is the company able to innovate?

offer you a competitive advantage. This is your opportunity to remind yourself of the value existing within your business.

Strengths need to be maintained, built upon or leveraged.

Quadrant II: Weaknesses –

Areas that are stand in the way in having you achieve your goals. These are areas of vulnerability from within your company.

These are areas that are within your control, but detract from your capacity to obtain or maintain a competitive edge. It is much easier to list your strengths than to acknowledge your weaknesses, but an objective assessment in this area will go a long way in moving your business forward.

Weaknesses might include lack of expertise, limited resources, lack of access to skills or technology, inferior service offerings or the poor location of your business. These are factors that are under your control, but for a variety of reasons are in need of improvement to effectively accomplish your marketing objectives.

Weaknesses detract from the value you offer or place you at a competitive disadvantage. These are areas you need to enhance in order to compete. The more accurately you identify your weaknesses, the more valuable the SWOT will be for your assessment.

Weaknesses need to be remedied or stopped.

Questions to Analyze Weaknesses

1. What are the least-profitable areas within the company?
2. In what areas is the company not able to recover costs?
3. Is the marketing/advertising effective?
4. Is the company focused?
5. Is the company able to attract competent employees?
6. What are the biggest expenditures for the company?
7. Is the company able to raise money when necessary?
8. Will the company be able to withstand price pressure from competitors?
9. Has the company been able to bring new ideas and services to its markets?
10. Do employees feel empowered to perform their best?
11. Do employees have faith in management?
12. Are the corporate governance standards high enough?
13. Is the company losing out to competitors on the service front?

Quadrant III: Opportunities

Areas that are supportive in having you achieve your goals. Areas of potential growth and possibility that exist in the external environment.

Opportunities may be the result of market growth, lifestyle changes, resolution of problems associated with current situations, positive market perceptions about your business or simply the ability to offer greater value that will create a demand for your products or services.

Usually, it is to your advantage to place a timeframe around potential opportunities. You must ask yourself, "How critical is my timing?"

Opportunities need to be prioritized and optimized.

Quadrant IV: Threats

Where do you see your external threats coming from? Threats are areas that affect your business' current or future growth and profitability. Threats can come from competitive forces, economic downturns, government interference and regulations, shifts in consumer behavior and buying

patterns and unexpected price increases by suppliers, among other factors. The better you are at identifying your actual and potential threats, the more effective you will be at developing strategies to mitigate their impact.

Threats need to be countered or minimized.

Preparing for SWOT Analysis:

A SWOT analysis should be done annually, prior to doing your marketing plan. I recommend including all of your key employees in this process. You will be surprised just how much information you will learn from this exercise.

Because this book is mostly focused on the marketing aspects of your business, I have kept the SWOT analysis mostly contained to this subject area. However, you may choose to make your SWOT analysis even broader in scope by visiting and examining all of the major areas in your business as well, including profitability, liquidity, cash flow, productivity and other human resource areas that are not directly related to marketing.

I suggest that you conduct your marketing SWOT analysis in the following manner:

1. Provide a comprehensive list of topics for consideration by your key people. Refer to the Marketing SWOT Analysis Categories for Consideration: Chart's I & II on pages 112 and 113.

2. Distribute the list to them at least four weeks in advance of the planning session.

3. Ask them to seriously consider the topics on the list, item by item, and make written comments as to their opinions and input.

Questions to Analyze Opportunities

1. Are there new technologies or services that the company can use to innovate?
2. Are there opportunities to expand into other related areas?
3. Are there acquisition opportunities?
4. Are there branch expansion opportunities?
5. Can the company use the Internet as a marketing channel?
6. Can the company spread its wings into other geographic areas?
7. Is there an opportunity to demand better prices from suppliers?
8. Are there opportunities to cooperate with non-competitive businesses?

Questions to Analyze Threats

1. Does the company have adequate reserves to withstand sudden changes in the environment?
2. Do government regulations threaten your business environment locally, statewide and nationally?
3. Is there trade union activity that could have an adverse effect?
4. Do the services the company offers have enough equity to withstand price competition?
5. Are competitors eating away at market share?
6. If the external economic environment becomes unstable, does the company have adequate resources to survive the downturn?
7. Is the company keeping up with technological advances?
8. Has the company been able to keep up with competitors in cyberspace?

4. It's imperative that they come to the planning session prepared.

5. Either have a professional consultant facilitate the meeting or do it yourself.

6. Hold the meeting off-site. You should allot one to two days.

7. Have someone take comprehensive notes. Tape record the session as well.

8. When the session is completed, develop an action plan from the points where you reached consensus.

9. Distribute the action plan to your key employees.

10. Delegate responsibilities for implementation.

Sample SWOT Analysis by Quadrants

(Macro-assessmant done by a service company)

1. Strengths
- Capabilities: knowledge
- Quick response
- Advertising
- Innovation
- Management
- Value

2. Weaknesses
- Gaps in capabilities
- Lack of competitive strength
- Sales force
- Customer attrition
- Branding
- Price

3. Opportunities
- Vertical markets
- Branch expansion
- Web advertising
- Relationships with non-competitive businesses

4. Threats
- Economic
- Fuel
- Reduction of market segment
- Lack of Web advertising

Action Plan to Address SWOT Analysis Findings:

Strengths/Findings:
Companies' employees are very knowledgeable and well trained.

According to customers, the response times to new accounts and to answer complaint calls has been excellent. We respond within 24 hours.

Advertising campaigns have been working well. Out tracking reports demonstrate a minimum 2:1 ROI on most media.

We have tested a number of new services with great success.

Our management team has been effective in motivating our employees.

Our customers find great value in our services.

Action Plan
Continue to add training programs

Try to improve response time to get same day.

Continue with same plan. Test cable TV over the next year.

Continue to assess effectiveness and acceptance of services by customers.

Continue to support management team. Increase meetings to weekly.

Continue reinforcing benefits.

Weaknesses/Findings:
We took on too many new projects this year and bit off more than we could chew.

We allowed our main competitors to outsell our services where we were most knowledgeable and competitively priced.

Our sales force is weak in expertise and in numbers.

Our customer cancellations are too high. We need to reduce them by 25 percent.

Action Plan
We need focus on our areas of expertise and limit new projects.

Put into place more sophisticated training programs for our sales force.

Hire a company to do screening. Commit more money to training. Hire two additional salespeople.

Set acceptable quota levels per serviceperson. Put incentives into place for employees to reduce cancellations. Put additional customer service training programs into place.

continued on next page

continued from previous page

Weaknesses/Findings: (continued)
Our image is stale, and we have not established a distinct identity.

Action Plan
Hire a marketing consultant to guide us in establishing an up-to-date brand identity.

Our profit margins are too low and we have not increased our prices in two. years

Implement a 5 percent, across-the-board price increase in season. Raise prices on all new starts by 8 percent.

Opportunities/Findings:
The company notices the potential for growth in the nursing home market.

Action Plan
It will commit one salesperson for two days per week to opening up this segment. The company will produce a brochure for this market. It will also purchase a database for use by the salesperson.

The company acknowledges the growth in the surrounding region and sees the population continuing to expand.

We will begin looking for an additional location immediately. Our goal is to have a new branch location in operation by this time next year.

We notice the growth of the Web and currently do not take advantage of PPC (Pay Per Click) advertising venues.

We will commit $1,000 per month to Web advertising.

We see the potential of additional business by developing referral relationships with other, non-competitive service contractors.

Write a letter to other service contractors and offer a 10 percent referral fee.

Threats/Findings:
An economic slowdown is currently under way. This is affecting our new sales, add-on service sales and renewals.

Action Plan
Retrain sales force in stating benefits and delivering value. Hire an additional customer service representative to call all accounts post-service. Mail customer satisfaction survey to clients.

If fuel costs continue to increase, this will have an even greater impact on profitability.

Tighten service routes. Impose a fuel surcharge on employees who take their vehicles home, or eliminate the practice altogether.

Threats/Findings: (continued)

During the past few years, one of our service segments has been severely affected by a number of forces. Some of these factors have been within our, control while others have been beyond our control.

We have noted that our competitors have been much more aggressive with their Web site designs, interactive sites and Web-based advertising campaigns.

Action Plan

Expand current market segments where we can identify our strengths. Look for additional supplementary market opportunities.

Update our Web site and commit to PPC advertising campaign.

Marketing SWOT Analysis Categories for Consideration – Chart I

Marketing:	Strengths	Weaknesses	Opportunities	Threats
Company image				
Level of planning				
Reputation for service				
Familiarity with market				
Market share				
Market growth				
Mission statement				
Directory advertising				
Radio advertising				
TV advertising				
Newspaper advertising				
Outdoor advertising				
Door hangers				
Direct mail				
Internet Web site				
Customer referrals				
Cross-selling				
Promotional brochures				
Sales brochures				
Newsletter				
Branding				
Vehicle signage				
Press releases				
Sales force				
Relationships w/contractors				
Public relations				
Community involvement				
Chambers of Commerce				
Rotary Clubs				
Lions Clubs				
Kiwanis Clubs				
Church groups				
Phone etiquette				
Customer service				
Competition:				
Dominant competitors				
Number of competitors				
Menu of services				

Marketing SWOT Analysis Categories for Consideration – Chart 2

Marketing:	Strengths	Weaknesses	Opportunities	Threats
Market Composition:				
Demographics				
Geographics				
Psychographics				
Socio-economic groups				
Population trends				
Mobility trends				
Economics:				
Growth of economy				
Affordability of service				
Pricing strategy				
Environmental/Technological:				
Environmental issues				
Pace of technological change				
Social/Cultural:				
Lifestyle trends				
Changes in consumer habits				
Business ethics				
Organizational:				
Leadership				
Senior management				
Mid-level managers				
Sales personnel				
Office staff				
Technicians (if service company)				
Employee retention				
Employee morale				
Customer service personnel				
General:				
Customer retention				
Service quality				
Value perception				
Reputation				
Training				
Political/Legal issues				

chapter 12
The Marketing Plan

This book addresses many individual topics relating to how to grow your business through your marketing. Up to this point, I have examined these segments one by one: from employees to customers, from budgeting to networking. The challenge is how to take the individual components and put them to work in a cohesive plan.

The vast majority of small- to medium-sized businesses run their marketing and advertising programs by the seat of their pants. This occurs for a number of reasons, not the least of which is a lack of understanding of how to go about the process.

Having a marketing plan entails much more than just putting together a budget or deciding what goes into your directory ad. Highly successful, progressive and growth-oriented companies have marketing plans. Large companies have plans with hundreds of pages; small companies can get by with a half-dozen sheets. Put your marketing plan in a three-ring binder. Refer to it at least quarterly, and revise as necessary. The bulk of your plan should focus on the coming year.

What is a Marketing Plan?

A marketing plan is a written document that puts into place the guidelines for your marketing and advertising programs over a fixed period of time (usually one year). It takes a comprehensive look at your company's soul, summarizes your core objectives and maps the methods of how you go about achieving your goals — and what precise actions you will take to attract customers to your products or services.

The marketing plan is your company's road map. It outlines, with specificity, how you get from here to there. It's the basis for all detailed operational planning each year. If you fail to use that map and go on your instincts, you stand the strong probability of getting lost. If your company is losing ground or has hit the proverbial revenue wall, it is most likely the result of improper planning.

What is the Difference Between a Marketing Plan and a Business Plan?

Your business plan is your master plan. It defines what your entire business is about and what your broader goals are. It encompasses more than marketing: It can include discussions of locations, staffing, financing, strategic alliances and more. Your business plan includes your vision statement. Your company's marketing plan exists within the body and context of your business plan. The two documents must be consistent.

Why Prepare a Marketing Plan?

1. Your marketing plan can help you focus your vision so that you can more effectively attract and retain customers.

2. Your marketing plan will save you money. You will use it to evaluate what worked and what didn't the previous year. It will give you the ability to track results and invest in programs based on hard data.

3. A marketing plan will save you time. By planning in advance and setting the pace and direction of your plan, you will not be forced to interrupt your schedule

at inopportune moments to come up with a last-minute ad or program.

4. A marketing plan will help secure financing. A well prepared and thought-out marketing plan, included as part of your business plan, will demonstrate to the lending institution that you have a specific strategy in place about how to attract and keep customers.

5. A marketing plan provides a foundation for your programs. It is your business' operational "bible." It's the thread that weaves together the individual programs into a cohesive unit.

6. Finally, your marketing plan provides a rallying point for your employees. It builds confidence and defines where you came from, where you are and where you are going. It allows your employees to feel part of a team engaged in an exciting and complicated joint endeavor. If you want your employees to feel committed to your company, it's important to share with them your vision of where the company is headed in the years to come. All of your employees should be exposed to the broader portions of your plan. Your employees will become motivated, feel valued and will become anxious to be involved in its successful implementation.

People don't always understand financial projections, but they can get excited about a well written and well thought-out marketing plan. You should consider releasing your marketing plan — perhaps in an abridged version — companywide. Do it with some fanfare and generate some excitement for the adventures to come. Your workers will appreciate being involved.

In this chapter, I will discuss how to go about putting together your own marketing plan, but I first want to state that there is no one way to do a marketing plan. It can be simple or complex, abbreviated or comprehensive. However, the more inclusive, methodical and focused the plan, the more power you will have over controlling the direction of your company.

Before you launch your next marketing campaign, you need to ask yourself a few questions:
- Have you prepared a sales forecast?
- Have you prepared a budget?
- Have you analyzed the market for your service or product?
- In forming your marketing message, have you described how your product or service will benefit your clients?
- Do you adequately differentiate your products and services from your competitors?
- Which media will you use in your marketing campaign?
- What type of customer service or support do you offer after the sale?

At this point, I would like to lay out two marketing plan options for you to consider: The first alternative is an outline for the abbreviated version; the second option is for the standard marketing plan with all the bells and whistles.

The Six Step Marketing Plan
Step I: The Summary
- Description of your business
- Listing of the products and services that you offer

- Business history
- Where your business stands today
- Where you envision it to be over the course of the next 12 months

Step II: The Market Review
- Description of your market
- Description of the business environment
- Why the market wants or values your services or products
- Is there enough money to be made with your products or services in your target market?
- Does your business benefit from any distinct marketing advantages?
- Are your products or services already well known?
- Do you have high customer loyalty?
- Do you have brand recognition?
- What are your competition's weaknesses, and how can you use those weaknesses to your advantage?
- Are there any foreseeable outside influences on your business?
- Have laws or statutes related to your business changed?
- Will future area construction affect your current traffic patterns?

Step III: Targeting Your Customers
- Who are your customers?
- What do your customers want?
- What motivates your customers to buy?
- What are the age, gender and educational levels of your customers?
- Where do they live?
- What is their socio-economic status?
- Do you know about any lifestyle characteristics?
- Are they from any specific social or ethnic groups?
- What are your customers' buying characteristics?
- Where does your target customer look to purchase your services or products?
- Who is the decision-maker or primary buyer?
- What is your target customer's motivation for buying?
- Do you have a niche(s) that you are trying to target?

Step IV: Stating Your Goals (Objectives)
Now that you have defined your customer, it is time to list your goals. These may include growing individual service segments or product sales by a specific amount. If you are a service business, for example, you may want to grow a residential or commercial market by a certain percentage. Make a list. Your goals should be reasonable, achievable and measurable, and have deadlines attached to them.

Step V: Meeting Your Goals (Methodology)
This is where all your product knowledge, service industry experience and assessment of what worked and what didn't come into play. This section of your plan will specify what you intend to do to accomplish your goals.

During this part of the plan, you are creating your messages, selecting your support materials, choosing your advertising venues and considering other marketing program options — all in preparation for meeting the upcoming year's goals. Which tools, support materials or media that you ultimately choose will depend on a number of factors, including your budget, target audience, goals and analysis of last year's data.

I thought it best to give you some

Setting Up Goals & Developing Methodologies to Meet Them

Goal	Methodology to meet goal
Differentiate company from the competition and create market awareness. for employees' use	Update company logo Develop company tagline Create mission statement commercial
Increase revenue in commercial business sector by 10 percent.	Design commercial brochures Join business networking groups Purchase targeted database Purchase ad in trade magazines Attend trade shows
Increase customer retention by lowering cancellation rates by 25 percent.	Hire a customer service representative Contact customers after all service calls Mail a quarterly newsletter Conduct annual quality assurance surveys
Increase annual new residential sales by 20 percent.	Make sure sales and service staff are in sync Create a new residential sales brochure Increase sales training sessions to twice monthly Purchase new sales tracking software Review price schedules

practical examples of the types of goals that you could be setting, within the body of your marketing plan, and the methodologies that should accompany them in order to accomplish your objectives. Please refer to the chart above.

I have also provided a number of advertising and marketing options for you to consider as part of your program. Please refer to the chart titled "Advertising Mediums to Consider" on the next page.

The Message

As important as it is to select the right vehicle for your message, it is equally important that your message be on target. Below, you will find a number of things to consider when putting together a cohesive message:

• Did you differentiate your service or product in the ad or promotional offering?

• Does your ad or promotion move the potential customer to action?

• What are the benefits that customers will receive from your products or services?

• Do you have testimonials from

customers about your products or services?

• What details can you provide about your pricing structure for your goods or services?

• What kind of guarantee are you willing to offer your customers?

Advertising Mediums to Consider

Directory advertising

Trade shows

Brochures

Networking

Door hangers

Outdoor advertising

Newspaper ads

Postcards

Newsletters

Home shows

Fairs

Special events

Web page

Email

Ezine ads

Fax broadcasts

Press releases

Articles

Movie ads

Radio

Television

Coupon books

Magazines

Trade journals

Seminars

Sponsorships

Charity events

Solicitation letters

Step VI: Putting Together a Budget

Budgeting is a critical part of your plan. For specific information about how to create a marketing budget, please refer to Chapter 5. Generally, small- to mid-sized companies spend between 3 percent and 9 percent annually on their marketing budgets. The smaller the company, the more that needs to be dedicated to advertising. In service industries like pest management, wildlife control and landscaping, target budgets should be 6 percent and 9 percent of annual projected revenues. Your budget should include all of your estimated marketing costs, including costs for printing and postage, labor expenses for attending trade shows, and any other expenses related to marketing or advertising promotions.

Testing Your Ideas

Use the 80/20 rule: Invest 80 percent of your advertising budget in proven promotions and 20 percent in testing new variations. Most businesses that adhere to this guideline find this minimal risk well worth the upside potential.

Who Should Have Access to Your Marketing Plan?

All the executives and managers in your company should have access. Unfortunately, most companies keep their marketing plans private for one of two reasons: Either they're too sparse, and the owners or executives would be too embarrassed by their lack of content, or they fear releasing too much proprietary information to their key people. This is an obvious trust issue.

You can't do a marketing plan without getting a lot of people involved. Feedback

from every facet of your company is key to making your plan a success. Your key people can provide realistic input on what's achievable and how your goals can be reached, and they can share any insights they have on any potential, as-yet-unrealized marketing opportunities — adding another dimension to your plan.

The Comprehensive Marketing Plan
Part I: The Summary
- Description of your business
- Listing of the products and services that you offer
- Business history
- Where your business stands today
- Where you envision it to be over the course of the next 12 months
- General recap of the plan

The Summary should be three pages or less in length.

Part II: The Table of Contents
The table of contents is a categorical listing of headings and sub-headings with page notations. This allows for easy access and quick reference of the desired materials.

Part III: The Market Review
A. Market Analysis
1. Demographic breakdown
2. Geographic breakdown
3. Psychographic breakdown
4. Socio-economic group breakdown

B. Needs Assessment
1. What needs are you filling?
2. Are you delivering value?

C. Trend Assessment
1. How is the business environment changing?
2. What new trends are occurring?
3. How do you plan to take advantage of emerging trends?

D. Market Growth
1. Assess the state of your market segments. Are they flat, growing or shrinking?
2. Do a SWOT (Strength, Weaknesses, Opportunities & Threats) analysis of your business and attach your findings here. (See the next chapter for details on how to perform this analysis).
3. Assess your major competitors' impacts and influences on the way you conduct your business. List all of your major competitors and individually describe their impact.
4. List all of your products and services individually, and list their benefits in terms of perceived value by the customer.
5. Identify four major areas where you would like your marketing plan to have the greatest impact.
6. Briefly summarize your past marketing successes and failures during the past year.
7. How do you expect to deliver your product or service to the market? Are your distribution channels prepared to meet the projected demands?

Part IV: Marketing Strategy
1. Write or include a mission statement. This should define your business' core values and objectives.
2. State all of your objectives for your marketing plan. This will be an

extensive list. Your goals should be reasonable, achievable and measurable, and have deadlines attached to them.

3. State your financial objectives for your marketing plan, individually and collectively.

4. List all of your individual target markets, and validate the reasons for their selection.

5. Include a positioning statement with your marketing plan. A positioning statement indicates who your customer is, what your product or service is and why people buy from you. This is usually accomplished in one sentence.

6. List all of your products and service offerings, along with your pricing strategy for each one.

7. How do you expect to promote your products and services? Be specific: Detail your strategy for each product or service offering.

8. How do you expect to get your product or service to the market?

9. What kinds of quality control systems do you have in place?

10. What kinds of marketing research do you plan to do?

Part V: Financials/Budgeting

1. You will commit _____ percent of revenue to your marketing budget.

2. You will attach a comprehensive budget along with this plan.

3. You will estimate the cost and projected profit on each marketing venue.

Part VI: Plan Implementation

1. Projected timetables to be included with this plan are based on individual projects, media commitments and seasonal revenue.

2. Attach a list of who will be responsible for the implementation of the individual projects.

3. The plan will be reviewed every _____ ___ and adjusted accordingly based on performance.

122

chapter 13
Focus Groups

In Chapter 11, I spoke about how to do a SWOT analysis on your business, which is an internal audit performed by your key people.

From time to time, it is good to get a controlled gut check from external forces — your customers. Therefore, you should conduct focus groups

A focus group is a market research tool where a small group of representative people are questioned regarding their opinions about their service or product preferences and/or their satisfaction levels. This targeted survey group is normally comprised of between six and 12 people. The discussion is most effective when facilitated through a trained, professional moderator.

When business is slow, management has more time to spend with customers to learn about their needs and wants and how they feel about their products or services. This will allow them the ability to make the appropriate improvements in their products and service delivery systems in the future.

Formal research done through focus groups will provide fresh perspectives of your customers' views in addition to providing an excellent forum for customer service evaluation and feedback.

These group gatherings also impress customers because they feel their opinions are being taken seriously. By conducting a focus group, you send a powerful message to your clients about your commitment to excellence in service delivery.

You can actually look at focus groups as laboratories, controlled environments where you can dissect the efficacy and marketability of your products and services. Focus groups also allow you an opportunity to test new service and product concepts and offerings.

Unlike the one-way flow of information in a one-on-one interview, focus groups generate data through the give-and-take of group discussion. Listening as people share and compare their different points of view provides a wealth of information, not just about what they think, but why they think the way they do.

Do Your Homework

Make certain that you define the objectives for your focus group before getting started. Focus groups may be used for the following purposes: gaining general input; determining program needs; the design and testing of new programs, services and products; measuring customer satisfaction levels; policy making and testing; organizational development and outcome evaluation.

Please take into consideration that the focus group's main purpose is to acquire information and data that will guide you in making future decisions. It must not be used as an immediate action facilitator without taking the time necessary to process the material.

Before getting started you need to ask yourself the following questions:

• What is my purpose for holding a focus group?

• What kind of information do I expect to obtain?

• How do I expect to use this information?

Getting People to Attend

• Set a convenient date, time and location for the meeting.

• You should seek group participants that reflect your typical customer. This is a key factor that will contribute to the validity and applicability of your focus group's

findings. Base the composition of the group upon the participants' age, gender and service and/or product usage. Focus group participants are generally selected on the basis of their use, knowledge, attitudes or feelings about the products, services or other test concepts that are the subject of the focus group. In selecting participants, the objective is to find individuals who can knowledgeably discuss the topics at hand and provide quality input that meets the specified research objectives.

- Call potential participants and invite them personally.
- When being recruited, potential participants receive a brief description of what the group will be about, as well as assurances that their participation is entirely voluntary and that their confidentiality will be protected. Focus group participants are often paid $25 to $50 for reimbursement of their time.
- For those who agree to attend, send a personal letter that confirms their participation and communicates the relevant details of the event.
- Make a reminder phone contact a few days before the event.
- Have a light meal or snack and beverages available.
- Offer gift cards as incentives for participation if you don't offer a stipend.
- Assure invitees that the session will last no longer than 90 minutes.

Location of Focus Group Setting

When setting up the session, it is important to give careful consideration to where you will be holding the focus group. The location should encourage relaxed participation and informal, spontane-ous feedback. The facility should be large enough and have comfortable seating.

Restaurants and similar locations are too distracting for optimal results. The facility should also be relatively quiet to minimize outside noises and distractions.

During the Session:

- Participants should be seated facing one another. A circular formation would be optimal, with the moderator/facilitator in the center.
- Get name tags for everyone.
- Keep the momentum going during the session — don't let the topics stray from the core issues, and make sure that you get the clear, concise answers that you are looking for.
- Explain that you will be recording the session for future reference and to assure accuracy.
- Don't allow any individual to try to dominate the discussion. Remember, you are looking for commonalities and consensus in responses as well as a diversity of opinions.
- Make sure that everyone gets a chance to speak.
- Listening closely and understanding clearly the response to your question is critical. Make certain that you understand what is being said.
- Allow the group enough time to think about the question before responding. Don't jump in prematurely.
- Once a response has been given, repeat and summarize it for acknowledgment.
- Do not get into a debate over responses to questions.
- Thank the attendees for their input at the end of the session and inform them that you will contact them with the action steps that you took resulting from their input.

Developing Questions for Focus Groups

All questions should be conversational and natural. They are usually short and open-ended, and you should only ask one question at a time.

• Remember, you will only have 60 to 90 minutes for questioning, so limit your key substantive questions to five or six at the most.

• Questions can deal with opinions (what an individual thinks about a topic), feelings (how they feel about a product or service), behaviors (how they react), knowledge (how much they know about an existing or future product or service), sensory perceptions (their physiological reactions and perceptions — what they see, feel, taste, touch or smell) or background data (such as demographics).

• Questions should not lead the respondent to a conclusion, and should be open-ended and neutral.

Clarifying Responses from Focus Groups

If a response is not clear to a question that you asked, you may wish to clarify it without influencing the outcome. For this, the use of a select number of probing questions is perfectly acceptable. You may, at your discretion, use any one of the following probes:

• Would you explain further?
• Would you give me an example of what you mean?
• Would you say more?
• Is there anything else?
• I don't understand. Would you explain further?

Post-session

• List your impressions of how the session went.
• Summarize your thoughts about the responses.
• Discuss your preliminary impressions with your key people and get their input.

Advantages of Focus Groups

• Provide useful input about current services and products.
• Provide useful input about future services and products.
• Generate information helpful in the structuring of consumer questionnaires.
• Help gather a wide range of information in a relatively short time span.
• The moderator can explore related, but unanticipated topics as they arise in the discussion.
• Do not require complex sampling techniques.
• Allow respondents to react to and build upon the responses of other group members.
• Decision-makers can readily understand the verbal responses of most respondents.

Disadvantages of Focus Groups

• The group may have one or more dominant people within it who may actually dissuade some other group member from making a full contribution.
• Difficult for moderator to interrupt once a discussion gets going.
• Bias from moderator.
• The sample is not necessarily a precise mirror of a target population, so the results cannot be evaluated statistically.

More Helpful Hints on Focus Groups

- Give participants the opportunity to express afterthoughts, or material they did not want to bring up in the group. Stick around at the end of the sessions. People will tell you things privately that are very valuable. Give them your business card, and invite them to contact you at any time if they have anything additional to offer.
- A style of extremely informal, relaxed playfulness, coupled with a professional seriousness of purpose, works best for most moderators. The worst style is one of formality.
- Make sure that the moderator addresses the participants of the group by their first names (after getting their permission, of course). Your moderator should also make the following statement at the beginning of your focus group's session: "If you find yourself having a totally different opinion than the rest of the group, I need to hear it because you will be representing a sizable portion of the people who just didn't happen to be here to support your view. So, I hope you will have the fortitude to speak up. If you don't speak up, an important view will not be represented."
- You can never do too much planning.
- Don't prejudge participants based on their appearance.
- Always videotape and/or audiotape the session and take written notes.

Advantages & Disadvantages of Other Surveying Methodologies

Advantages

Mail Surveys
No interviewer bias
Anonymous returns (if preferred)
Can be completed at leisure

Telephone Surveys
Easy to administer
Quick
Allows for reaction and some in-depth interviews.
Questions can be modified

Disadvantages

Postage can be expensive
Low response rates
Take longer
Must be short
Responses may be misinterpreted
No moderator to guide respondent

Possible invasion of privacy
High non-response rate because of not-at-homes, refusals and answering machines

chapter 14
Vertical Marketing

Vertical marketing is defined as a service, product or promotion targeted at a particular industry or business segment. Vertical marketing can open doors and tap into niche markets, where the competition may be less. Many times, these niche markets are ignored by large companies. A creative marketer may find it easier to establish brand recognition in a vertical market.

Acquiring industry-specific knowledge will also give you an edge up on competitors that are more horizontally diffuse. By establishing knowledge in vertical markets, you also build credibility within those sectors.

The messages that you deliver to these specific market segments should be more focused, resulting in greater acceptance by the targeted audience. Another benefit of concentrating on vertical markets is that marketing budgets tend to go farther and produce greater ROI because you have a more detailed understanding of your target market and the media that support it. A common mistake is the failure to understand the verticals you choose to target.

Vertical marketing is a great way to expand your current customer base. It is an underutilized, immensely profitable marketing opportunity for businesses. Customers in these market niches are willing to pay more to vertical marketers because they provide industry-specific programs and products. They are supported by people with industry-specific knowledge and experience and consequently have developed a unique standing within their niche.

Industry professionals also tend to listen to their peers (other member businesses within their vertical segment), and a recommendation or endorsement can help spread a program's popularity within a specific market or industry segment. Trade publications, for example, are more likely to give ink to a press release that targets their focus. There are also numerous link-up opportunities if you are able to illustrate how your product or service appeals to a specific industry.

Most general marketing applications can be effectively targeted at specific industries or verticals with just a little modification and creativity. The idea is to adapt your current marketing materials — and with a little creativity, make them unique or beneficial to a specific group of people. Often all that is required are changes to your ad copy and presentations.

Increasing revenue and decreasing costs are the results of an effective vertical strategy. Verticals allow us to increase our win rate by increasing revenue as well as decreasing the cost of sales. A major benefit of a vertical strategy is effectiveness and efficiency in sales and marketing. With every sales and marketing campaign, we gain experience and knowledge. We learn about our services and products; we learn about the prospect's industry, business and people. This experience and knowledge is available in all marketing campaigns, but with horizontal advertising and marketing programs, the impact and results are more diffuse and difficult to measure.

With a vertical focus, each campaign contributes to knowledge that will help us with future campaigns. Product and service knowledge reveals how our products and services can better serve specific needs, or

how best to present a product or service to a targeted market.

What we learn about a company and its people contributes to our understanding of the industry. Most industries have a "personality" that is common throughout their members.

When we have a vertical strategy, we have an advantage. If we have no vertical focus, the tables are turned. If we don't have vertical focus, we will be at a disadvantage in every sales campaign because it will be extremely rare for us not to be facing a vertically focused competitor. When we win with a vertical focus, each new customer has the potential to become a reference for all future prospects.

When we become more effective at closing sales and selling products within a vertical market, we increase our ability to gain additional prospects. Our close rate goes up because we are doing a better job, and we are selling to prospects where we already know their industry, needs and issues.

Furthermore, we have increased credibility with the prospect — and we can add value from the point of our first call. With experience, we can do a better job of setting traps for our competition. We can set the bar high, so only we can pass the test.

What an effective sales and marketing effort means is a lower cost of sales. We take less time learning the needs of a specific prospect and less time preparing for sales calls. With tightly focused vertical marketing programs, we can spend less time and money to get the prospects that have the highest odds of leading to business.

Strategic Planning for Vertical Markets: 15 Tips to Get You Started

1. Construct an offer that is unique to an industry or group of people. Develop a campaign surrounding that specific market.
2. Make your message more precise because your market is more restricted.
3. Modify your current promotional materials to be in-sync with the targeted market segment.
4. Seek and use testimonials from group members. Potential customers value input from their peers.
5. Write columns for trade publications.
6. Offer niche discounts.
7. Focus your ad on a specific sector.
8. Attend industry-specific trade shows, fairs and events.
9. Link your Web site to targeted industry Web sites.
10. Advertise in vertical trade journals, newsletters and magazines.
11. Join vertical trade groups and organizations.
12. Link your Web site to Chambers of Commerce.
13. Sponsor functions in vertical markets.
14. Hold informative breakfasts or luncheons to introduce your product or services.
15. Send out a direct-mail solicitation. These are more effective in vertical markets.

Limitless Opportunities

There are endless opportunities that exist in vertical markets. Consider developing specialized, targeted programs for the vertical markets that offer the greatest potential for your business' products and services. Vertical marketing should become a part of every company's strategic marketing plan. Preparing for this positioning requires focus, an in-depth understanding of a niche and a keen ability to differentiate your services.

The result of your efforts will be realized by growing revenue streams and greater profitability.

Sample Vertical Market Listing

Hospitals • Doctor offices • Dialysis units • Outpatient surgical centers • Nursing homes • Medical laboratories • Hotels • Motels • Bed & breakfasts • Restaurants • Supermarkets • Government buildings • Military bases • Schools • Banks • Churches • Synagogues • Veterinary hospitals • Animal groomers • Animal boarding facilities • Construction Industry •Health Clubs

Three Examples of Vertical Marketing Strategies for the Service Sectors

Veterinarians and Groomers (For the Pest Management Industry)
This category presents a great way to exemplify the power and opportunity that exists within vertical markets:

1. Secure a database listing all of the veterinary hospitals and animal groomers in your area.

2. Prepare a brochure specifically for this market segment, stressing your knowledge, experience and environmental responsibility.

3. Once you get the account, offer them a professional courtesy fee for referring their clients. When you offer a professional courtesy discount for patient referrals, you will watch your flea and tick jobs come rolling in.

4. Leave behind a point-of-purchase information display that sits on the countertop for clients to avail themselves.

5. Once you get the account, ask for a testimonial. Go after other similar accounts. Eventually, you will become a specialist in this market segment.

Church Groups & Synagogues (All Industries)
Solicit church groups and synagogues. Advertise in their newsletters. Offer to tithe back a percentage of revenue in exchange for permission to solicit their congregations' databases. Ask for a personal endorsement from a senior member of the congregation. It will go a long way in building credibility and revenue.

Healthcare Industry (All Industries)
If you are servicing (or considering servicing) a hospital, nursing home or rehabilitation facility, there are a number of things you can do to optimize interaction with this vertical marketplace:

1. Make sure that you have the appropriate materials targeted for this sector. Focus on the environmental responsibility aspect of your products and services.

2. Attend health fairs and join trade organizations that cater to this group.

3. Seek testimonials from executives in this sector.

4. Advertise in newsletters and magazines that focus on this market segment.

5. Advertise to the employees of these organizations in their in-house newsletters, featuring special discounts.

chapter 15
Public Relations

Before going into the numerous ways in which incorporating a media-focused public relations (PR) program into your company can be useful, I would first like to define the concept. PR resides under the umbrella of your broader marketing communications program, beneath the subcategory of promotion. Its purpose is to create and promote a positive image and build goodwill by gaining public trust, understanding and acceptance. Public relations efforts may be conducted through the media or through numerous other networking outlets.

Advertising and media-focused public relations differ in one fundamental way: You pay for advertising. PR is free. Media-based PR offers third-party legitimacy that advertising does not.

A public relations strategy should be an important part of your overall annual planning process, and the effectiveness of your public relations program should be evaluated annually as part of your SWOT analysis.

If you ran a PR campaign last year, review what worked and what didn't. What got you successful coverage? Which media outlets and journalists used your stories? Assess the amount of coverage that you received vs. the amount of unsuccessful attempts.

Now: On to current day.

Putting Together a Successful PR Program

1. Consider your business objectives. Ask yourself these questions: What part(s) of your business do you want to focus on? What do you want to say about it? What stories do you think the media would be interested in covering?

2. Evaluate opportunistic scenarios. Do you have a new service or product that would generate interest from the public's perspective? Has there been a core shift or innovation in your industry that is so evolutionary (or revolutionary) that it would generate public interest (such as the green movement)?

3. Develop a PR plan for the upcoming year. Include timelines, services and products that you expect to feature, press contacts (create a comprehensive list of all the news outlets in your area, including newspapers, business journals, radio and TV stations) and upcoming events.

Creating a Media Contact List

You should maintain a current media contact list that includes the following information: Name of media outlet, contact name, contact's title, phone, fax and email, street address, format/frequency (print, broadcast, weekly, monthly, etc.), deadlines and details of each interaction you've had with the publication or media.

Creating a Press Release

Throwing together a few sentences with some copy and contact information does not create an effective press release. You must take the time and make the effort to put together a professional press release if you want to have a shot at having it published. If you do so, you just might be surprised when you see it appear in print or have the contact person call to inform you that they intend to cover your story.

Remember, your press release should not be simply a veiled product or sales pitch. Why? It's because another name for a press release is a news release. If your material is viewed as advertising, it will be

rejected out-of-hand and turned over to the advertising department.

The purpose of a press release is to inform and educate, not to sell.

When writing your release, you need to consider writing it from a perspective as if you were the reader. Make sure your release is newsworthy. You should be asking and answering the following questions:

- Who is it about?
- What is it about?
- When will the event take place? (Or when will the product or service be available?)
- Where is it going to take place? (Or where can I get the product or service?)
- Why is it important?
- How will it benefit me?

One of the key elements in the press release is a captivating headline. It needs to be bold, inviting and meaningful. If it doesn't make the editor stop and take note, your press release will find its way into the circular file or be deleted.

Once the headline is completed, you are ready for the body text (see above: who, what, why, when, where and how). Make sure to keep it simple; confine your copy to one side of one page. Never go beyond that. If you are doing the press release to have media coverage for an event, just put enough information in to grab the editor's attention and to peak his interest in contacting you for more information.

Once your press release is completed, make sure that you send it to the correct editor. This is key. Consider the audience that you are trying to reach and submit your release accordingly. If you have any questions about who to submit it to, I suggest that you contact the media outlet

and ask for some direction.

Before you send out your press release, be sure to proofread it. Keep your sentences and paragraphs short. A paragraph should contain no more than four sentences. It should be written in a word-processing program and checked for spelling and grammar errors. The release should be factual, not hyped: Don't use a sales pitch, as it will ruin your credibility with the editor.

Now it is time to format your release. There is a standard format that you should use when preparing your release. Editors expect that this basic format will be followed. Ignoring it can decrease the chances of your press release from being considered. (See sample press release format on page 139.)

Now that all is completed, you can distribute your press release.

Other PR Opportunities
1. Promotions/Achievements

Most newspaper and business publications have a column featuring promotions, appointments and achievements. Write a press release, including the name of the individual as well as a list of his accomplishments. Be sure to include some brief informational ("promotional") material about your company. For example:

John Jones of XYZ Co., one of the area's most trusted names in service management, has recently been promoted from service technician to service manager. Jones has been with XYZ for 15 years and has been dedicated to upholding the company's service credo of "outstanding service every visit."

Now, you may be saying to yourself that there is absolutely no way that a newspaper will print that kind of self-promoting

material. Well, think again. It actually happened in a small local interest community newspaper. While major media outlets will probably edit out most of the pap, what do you have to lose?

2. Contributing Editor
Many community newspapers are always looking for interesting fill material. Contact the newspaper and find out which editor is responsible for special-interest columns.

Offer to write a seasonal column featuring the topics related to your services or products. Remember, your focus must be on how the consumer will benefit.

Prior to calling the paper, be sure that you have your "pitch" straight. They will be certain to want to know what qualifies you as an expert. The more credentials you have, the likelier you are to be considered. You might mention the number of years that you have been servicing your community, for example.

3. Guest Expert
If you are in a market that has a local talk radio or cable television station, contact the show host and offer to appear as an expert. You can pitch the public interest aspect of your product or service. Once again, be certain to have all of your "ducks in a row" before you call.

4. Guest Speaker
Speaking opportunities offer another avenue for generating exposure. When planning your PR activities for the year, research conferences, organizations and trade shows for opportunities to speak or to be a member of a panel discussion.

5. Events/Trade Shows
If you're hosting an event or attending a trade show, here are some things to consider:
- Pitch publications with your news for advance coverage of the event.
- Send out a media advisory the week before the event to encourage local press to "save the date."
- See the Media Advisory Template on page 141.
- Obtain the pre-registered press list from trade show organizers, and set up on-site interviews with appropriate reporters. Discuss announcements being made, future plans, industry trends and other relevant topics.
- Bring plenty of press kits.

Follow this "who, what, when, where and why" format to help get your message across to the media as quickly and clearly as possible.

6. Other Types of PR
Taking a broader view of PR, it can also be seen as anythng that you do to enhance your company's credibility and image in the mind of the public/consumer. After all, it *is* called public relations. Therefore, the sponsorshp of local teams, organizations, community events, charitable and church functions, etc., are all included under its vast umbrella. I encourage you to broaden your PR perspective to include this planning as well.

When the Media Comes Calling:
Another Important Part of the PR Equation
This strategic plan will prepare you for when a hostile reporter calls or shows up for your side of a breaking story:

Sample Press Release

Service Management Company, Inc.
1234 Any Road
City, State, Zip Code
Phone Number, Fax Number, Email Address

Your Letterhead

FOR IMMEDIATE RELEASE

Top of Release

Contact Information:
  Contact Person
  Company Name
  Phone
  Fax
  Email

Contact Information

Local Pest Management Company First in Region to Offer Green Service Options

Headline

The headline needs to "grab the attention" of the editor. It should be in bold type and a font that is larger than the body text. Capitalize every word with the exception of "a," "an," "the" or any word that is three characters or less.

Body Copy

<City>, <State>, <Date> — The first paragraph should be written in a clear and concise manner. It must be able to invite the reader to read further into the text. Remember, don't make your press release a sales pitch or it will end up in the "circular file." Answer the questions "who," "what," "when," "where," "why" and "how." Keep your sentences and paragraphs short; a paragraph should be no more than four sentences.

Final Paragraph

The last paragraph before the company information should read: For additional information on (put in the subject of this release), contact "name" or visit www.yoururl.com.

Closing

ABOUT <COMPANY> - Include a few sentences about your company along with the services or products provided.

1. Develop a crisis management plan. Communicate it to your employees, and be certain that they understand it.

2. Designate one person as the company spokesperson. This individual should be a good communicator as well as knowledgeable. All employees should be instructed to direct all media inquiries to this individual.

3. Never fail to respond to a media inquiry. If you do, you may find the media outlet using one of these two negative and "guilty by unresponsive" quotes: "We contacted XYZ company, and they didn't return our calls." "The company had no comment." Both of these responses, when uttered by a

reporter, can have a devastating impact on your business. In the mind of the public, you are judged guilty by your silence.

4. Respond to media inquires in a timely manner. Remember, newspapers as well as radio and television stations have deadlines. If you want your side of the story told, you had better respond promptly.

5. Use your resources. Of course, it is imperative to act judiciously when responding to media inquiries. Whenever possible, try to buy the company some additional time by saying: "I'll have someone get right back to you." If a reporter shows up at your office, ask him to have a seat and you will have someone

Differences Between Media-Based Public Relations & Advertising

Public Relations	Advertising
Free media coverage.	Media placement paid for.
Company identified as part of story.	Company name prominently displayed.
Product/Service sales message is a byproduct. Message is informative. Intention is for good will generation. Company becomes personalized.	Service/Product sales message prominent and overt.
The media control the outcome of. the message.	You control the outcome of the message
Uses networking opportunities, such as community involvement, speaking opportunities and sponsorships, as well as the mass media.	Uses the media.
Message perception viewed as unbiased by public.	Message viewed as biased.
The media control when the message is delivered to the public	You control when the message is delivered.

with him shortly. Then call your lawyer, your national trade association or your state trade association, all of which are good places to start.

6. Don't panic. If you've preplanned well, you can almost go on autopilot.

Planning Pays Off

Having one strategic, proactive plan for generating positive press and another reactive plan to prepare for the unexpected can go a long way in not only generating new assets but protecting existing ones as well.

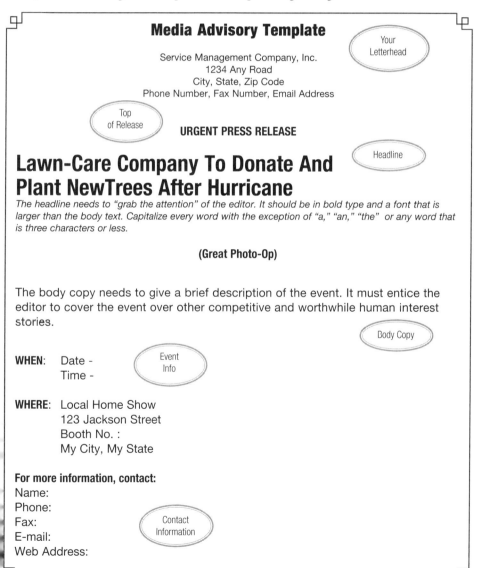

Media Advisory Template

Your Letterhead

Service Management Company, Inc.
1234 Any Road
City, State, Zip Code
Phone Number, Fax Number, Email Address

Top of Release

URGENT PRESS RELEASE

Lawn-Care Company To Donate And Plant NewTrees After Hurricane

Headline

The headline needs to "grab the attention" of the editor. It should be in bold type and a font that is larger than the body text. Capitalize every word with the exception of "a," "an," "the" or any word that is three characters or less.

(Great Photo-Op)

The body copy needs to give a brief description of the event. It must entice the editor to cover the event over other competitive and worthwhile human interest stories.

Body Copy

WHEN: Date -
Time -

Event Info

WHERE: Local Home Show
123 Jackson Street
Booth No. :
My City, My State

For more information, contact:
Name:
Phone:
Fax:
E-mail:
Web Address:

Contact Information

chapter 16
The Media & The Message

Directory Advertising

If you are a service company, chances are that your directory advertising is an important part of your advertising strategy. I said this before but I want to say it again: Never commit any more than 50 percent of your advertising budget to your directory program.

I say this for a very good reason. Directory advertising is a passive medium. What this means is that you have to wait until someone comes looking for you. It's unlike most other advertising vehicles, where you consciously place your message actively in front of consumers to get their attention.

That said, if you are a service company, you can't ignore the value of this advertising resource. Directory shoppers have three characteristics in common when they reach for their phone books:

1. They are event-driven.

2. They are information gatherers.

3. A significant percentage of them are ready to buy.

Directory User Habits

• Approximately 48 percent of the consumers referencing the Yellow Pages have a decision to make at the time of the reference.

• Yellow Page consumers with one name in mind still look at an average of four ads before making a purchase.

• Approximately 42 percent of print Yellow Page consumers make a purchase after referencing the Yellow Pages.

Things You Need to Know About Directory Advertising

A couple of givens here:

1. Size matters — period. The larger the size of the ad, the more attention you get (more about this shortly).

2. The bigger your ad budget per directory, the better the deal you can negotiate.

As you know, the goal of the directory salesperson is to get you to spend as much as possible of your overall advertising budget with his company. Today, that includes selling you Web directory links and pay-per-click advertising options.

Ask for Independent, Third-Party Research

Almost every directory salesperson will tell you that his directory is the best or is more effective at reaching your customers. Make them put up or shut up.

Most publishers track usage statistics for their directories, so ask to see the results. The data can range from heading use in a specific directory to measured call counts for one or more display ads under a particular category. Request a copy of the study itself. You want to make certain that it was performed by an independent, third-party research firm.

Negotiating the Rates

Most small businesses just assume that because of their size, the rates they are quoted are fixed and immovable. While in some rare instances this is true, for the most part the salesperson has some wiggle room. Don't settle for the first price offered. Play hardball: You know what you can afford, and you need to know you're buying the most competitive ad size within your budget.

Of course, the rep will try to use the old "If you don't sign today, you may lose your position" game. But, in more

instances than not, he will move toward your position. Remember, he wants the sale as much as you want the ad.

Oh yes, if after is all said and done your salesperson won't budge much on reducing the price of the ad, ask about having him throw in a second ad gratis. Sometimes this strategy will work, as well. Directory studies have shown that a second, smaller display ad could increase call volume significantly, particularly where there are crowded headings. The salesperson could offer anything from a small display to an in-column ad.

Positioning

As I stated earlier, size matters. Go for the largest ad you can afford. Bigger ads attract more customers and get better placement. The larger the ad, the more forward in your section the ad will appear. Double truck ads rule (two full pages, side-by-side). However, it is still possible to be the second or third double truck ad in your section. That is because the position of your ad is guided by the size of the ad and the length of time that your ads have appeared in that section. If a competitor doesn't renew for an ad this year but wants it next year, it will fall to last position (for that ad size) because it will have lost its seniority.

Advertising in the Big Book and/or the Competitors?

Each locale has one main directory and a number of smaller directory competitors. The big book is usually the most widely used, but many times the smaller secondary directories get used quite frequently — and their rates are significantly lower. Their representatives have more flexibility to

discount prices, so don't be afraid to go for it. You may be able to get good positioning at good rates.

Ad Design

This is one area that totally perplexes me. Companies will spend thousands of dollars per year on their directory advertising placements, yet have their ads prepared by the art departments of the directory companies just to save a few dollars. It just doesn't make a heck of a lot of sense, and that is why most directory advertising looks alike. Your ads are competing with numerous ads and messages. Doesn't it seem logical to have your ad designed by a graphic artist of *your* choosing? Someone who will work with you based upon the input that you provide regarding your business segment, your differentiation points and your goals?

A couple of tips regarding design. First, white space matters. If your ad is too cluttered, it will be ignored. Second, if you have a choice between upsizing your ad or going with a smaller ad in color, go with the larger ad. Third, if you have to go with a smaller ad, and there are a lot of competitors on the same page as you, getting your ad to stand out with color or a white knockout would be preferable.

Coupon Use

Directory representatives are usually anxious to sell you coupons as an up-sell. I just thought it might be interesting to mention that little or no data exists to prove how well coupons deliver new customers. It is up to you to be able to evaluate the value.

If you decide to go with a coupon, here are a few tips:
• Make a specific offer, like free initial

service with annual agreement or a dollar amount or percentage off.

• State the conditions, such as "new customers only."

• Print an expiration date on the coupon, usually the same date as the directory expires.

• Make certain to prominently state that you offer a coupon in your main ad.

• Print the words "one coupon per customer," and, if applicable, "not valid with any other offer."

• If you are purchasing coupons in multiple directories, print a code on each coupon so you can track the performance of specific directories.

• Track all your coupons so you can evaluate the success of the program.

One other point to make about coupons: Try to negotiate for their inclusion as part of your directory advertising package.

Call Tracking

One of the biggest problems and challenges with directory advertising is the ability to track the calls coming in and to know which directories produced which leads. This can be achieved through gaining access to a special phone number that you use in each directory ad. The number is available from most publishers and ties into your regular phone line. Calls on the number are tracked, and you get a monthly report. Call tracking numbers are a great tool to measure the effectiveness of your directory advertising.

Design Tips for Directory Ads

Why is the design element so important to the success of your directory ad? Because prior to referring to the directory, 33 percent of users do not have a specific business name in mind of where to make a purchase. Potential customers with one name in mind will still consider an average of four ads, after opening the directory but before making a purchase. Finally, directory shoppers will spend an average of 30 seconds looking at an ad that attracts them before moving on to viewing the next ad. If your ad doesn't attract their attention in the first place, you're toast.

A Few Good Tips
The Headline
• Should grab readers' attention and get them to react.

Example: You Have a Problem? We Have the Solution! And We'll be There Today!

As you might have noticed, this headline differentiates the service provider from its competition by focusing on a major consumer desire to have the problem solved as soon as possible.

The Body
• Should contain graphics
• Leave significant white space (more difficult, of course, with smaller ads)
• Have differentiation points
• Stress benefits
• Make an offer
• Call the reader to action.

Important Considerations
• Does the ad cite specific products and services offered?
• Does the business list credit cards?
• Does the business list free estimates and consultations?

- Does the ad make it clear why the user should contact this business instead of another competitor?
- How long has the business been around? Does the ad say it?
- Do you list your credentials and professional organization affiliations?
- Are you using bursts and callouts to garner attention for your major points?
- If your business is customer service-focused, does your ad say it and convey it?
- Does your ad shout value through its pictures and words?
- Does the ad want to make the customer contact your company?
- Is the ad easy to read?
- Don't forget to proofread your ad. Don't assume anything — your business depends on it.

The Two Most Important Things You Need to Know about Directory Advertising

1. Plan, Plan, Plan in Advance! The biggest mistake companies make regarding their directory advertising is waiting until the last minute to decide about the size and placement. If you create a marketing plan and advertising budget each year, directory deadlines should be incorporated into the plan. If you don't have a marketing plan, keep a separate binder with all of your deadline dates highlighted in red. Make sure that you are keeping track of your deadline proof commitment dates and not the directory's publishing dates.

2. Track, Track, Track! Tracking your directory results is key to your success. As I said before, this is an area where many companies falter. It's imperative to track as many incoming calls as possible. When tracking systems are in place, they allow you to make prudent decisions regarding your upcoming placements based upon fact and not on conjecture. More companies than not renew their annual directory advertising based on the fear that not doing so will result in less business. The fact is that many companies continue to put their budgets into directories that are not producing results.

If you are not getting a 2:1 ROI (return on investment) on your directory advertising from each book, then I strongly suggest that you take one of the following actions:

- Downsize your ad significantly in that book, and put the difference into a book that is giving you 2:1 or better results.
- Pull your ad out of that directory completely and put it in another effective directory area.
- Pull the money out of the area with poor results and test a new area.
- Cancel the directory that is producing poor results and put your dollars into an entirely different advertising/marketing area.

Direct Marketing

For the purpose of defining direct marketing in this book, I will refer to it in its most simplistic form to make its core definition easy to understand. Although forms of direct marketing can be used to solicit business in the electronic media through infomercials and home shopping networks as well as using tear-out coupons in magazines, I specifically am excluding those forms of direct marketing in my simplified definition. In this section, I will be focusing exclusively on the most widely identified direct marketing tools: direct mail print campaigns using various types of mailers and door hangers.

Definition of Direct Marketing

Direct marketing is a promotion apparatus that allows focused messages to be received by a targeted audience. The main difference between direct marketing and other promotions is that you can closely qualify your audience to deliver messages that appeal to their specific needs. Direct mail entails the practice of delivering promotional messages directly to potential customers on an individual basis, as opposed to through a mass medium (for the most part — except for those mentioned above).

Some Direct-Mail Rules to Live By

Target Your Customer

Do your homework. Your targeted customer will mirror your current customer base. You can have a right-on offer but if it doesn't reach the right target audience, you have just wasted your time and money.

Take a Strategic Approach

Start your research by looking at the direct mail you receive every day to come up with ideas to make your mailings more attractive. Think creatively to grab your potential customer's attention. Focus on a key idea and make it worthwhile. Mailings that offer a special promotion encourage a response.

Creating the Message

- Personalize them as much as possible. Type or print the addresses rather than using standard labeling.
- Use a compelling headline that spells out the benefits you're offering.
- Make a knock-out offer that makes the recipient want to call.
- Make sure your body copy really is easy to read. Use colors, fonts and placement to make sure that this information is impossible to overlook.
- Include your telephone number, address, fax number and email address. Different recipients often prefer different methods of making contact. Allow your customers to reach you in the way that feels most comfortable for them.
- Use every inch of space effectively. Refine your ideas to a core message, and select a powerful image that supports it.
- Include an expiration date.
- Make sure to state, "This offer not valid with any other offers or coupons."
- You also may want to include a disclaimer in your mailer that states any exclusion, like "For new customers only."

The Direct-Mail Line-up

These types of direct-mail promotion venues give you many options to work with.

Brochures give you the space to go into a bit more detail than with postcards, which only allow for a hit-and-run message. You can present your offer on a heavier stock or a glossy stock. They will also allow you the space to make good use of color graphics and text to capture the attention of the potential customer. If you are using a brochure, you can eliminate the need for using an envelope by addressing it on the back panel and simply closing it with a self-stick tab.

Catalogs, of course, will allow you to go into great detail if you are selling products. You may also include a coupon with an incentive to purchase inside of your catalog.

Newsletters are another terrific tool for marketing to your internal customers as well as to some targeted potential external customers. With newsletters, you have the space to include some inside background information about your company. You can also include coupons and other types of incentive offers that will call the customer to action.

There is one shortcoming with using these types of venues: They involve increased costs of postage, processing and printing. They are also more time-consuming because you can't run the bulkier items through the same machinery as a flat envelope or postcard. Typically, expensive mailings like these are sent to existing customers.

Postcards are one of the most popular ways of doing a direct-mail campaign. They are simple to design and are the least-expensive to print and to mail. The big challenge with postcards is that the surface area that your message is printed on is limited, so your headline and offer have to be succinct and capturing. This also works to your advantage because it doesn't require a lot of the customer's time trying to figure out what it is that you are trying to say. If you decide to go with this venue, I strongly recommend that you go with the oversized postcards because the smaller ones seem to stick to other pieces of mail and may also get lost in the sea of "junk mail."

Mailers are nothing more than letters in envelopes. For this type of marketing promotion, I would not include more than three letters (promotional offers) in one envelope, because that is about the weight limit of a 1-oz. mailing (including the envelope). When you choose this type of venue, it will allow you more opportunity to present a greater amount of detail and information about your products and services. You can also add a reply envelope to increase responses. However, when using this type of format, it's important that you place a strong teaser message on the exterior of the envelope so that the customer will not be able to resist opening it.

Snap Mailers

These kinds of direct-mail pieces are distinctive envelopes that unfold to disclose the offer. The sides of the envelopes are perforated. The recipient tears along the sides and reveals the message inside or removes a concealed sheet of paper. Many credit card companies promote special offers using this form of direct-mail marketing.

Dimensional Mail

This is the most creative of all the direct-mail venues. It will use unique sizes and shapes in its effort to attract attention. It may be shipped in a box or a tube to stimulate the person to open it. Dimensional mail can also include something mailed with your logo or name branded on it, like a pen, magnet, calendar or fly swatter. It is the most expensive of all of the direct-mail mediums to produce and mail. Therefore, you shouldn't send it to unqualified prospects or names from an outdated mailing list.

Self-mailers

Self mailers are tri-folded, single sheets of paper. The offer is printed on both sides, but there is room for the address on one of the exterior panels. It is sealed with an adhesive tab. This type of mailer is very inexpensive to produce and mail, but it could get damaged during its trip to the customer.

Door Hangers: A Direct Marketing Goldmine

Door hangers are one of the cheapest, most effective forms of direct marketing a print campaign can have. Door hangers command more attention because they are not lumped in with the rest of the mail.

Unlike direct mail, which sits in mailboxes waiting to be picked up and brought in the house, door hangers wait on doorknobs, where they're much more likely to receive special attention. Yes, they have to be hand-delivered, but you get to skip the cost and middlemen involved in stamping, addressing and shipping conventional direct mail.

There are a few different ways of using door hangers as part of your marketing strategy.

Clover-leafing: Have your services personnel drop off the door hangers to adjacent homes while they are on their regular service routes.

Making use of down time: Have your service personnel deliver to homes or businesses in their service areas, when business is slow.

I would just like to comment about having your service personnel deliver the door hangers. Make certain that you have a quality control system in place to make certain that the door hangers are being delivered. It is a good idea to have a service manager do an unannounced check-up from time to time. Your employees must understand that it is part of their job responsibility to deliver these door hangers.

Another way of having your service staffs cooperate is by attaching a reward system to any sales that you pick up as a result of the referral. If a customer calls and asks for service, offer the serviceperson a 10 percent referral fee. If the customer calls to make an appointment with a salesperson to come out and talk about the service and the salesperson closes the sale, split the commission between the salesperson and the serviceperson.

Hire a professional delivery service to target new areas: This is not very expensive and makes a lot of sense to me.

Track, Track, Track!

By definition, direct marketing and direct mail require close attention to response and close ratios. This is perhaps one of the easiest methodologies to control because you will have direct responses to specific offers.

Projecting Response Rates: One Formula

The easiest way to calculate your response rate is to work backward. Let's assume that your goal is to attract 1,000 new customers to your company. Next, let's assume that there will be a 2 percent lead response rate to your campaign. Of that 2 percent response rate, let's further

conjecture that 50 percent of the respondents will purchase your services or products.

Based upon this formula, you will need a mailing list containing 10,000 names to wind up with 100 customers: (10,000 * 2 percent * 50 percent = 100). Response rates will vary depending upon the accuracy of the list purchased and type and attractiveness of the offer. Direct mail professionals often use a 1 percent to 2 percent response rate as their benchmark for a successful campaign.

(For an example of how to calculate ROI for a direct-mail campaign, see page 155.)

Purchasing Lists

There are two main types of lists that can be purchased:

Compiled mailing lists contain information from public records and sources such as the phone book, courthouse records, bankruptcy filings, mortgage deed records and others.

Response lists contain names of individuals who have responded to an offer either through the mail or through other means of mass communication.

You must determine which list is better suited to your needs. Compiled lists are perfect for businesses that need to target a well-defined market — families with household incomes of $50,000 who live within 10 miles of your store, for example. This is good news if you understand the demographic profile of your customers because compiled lists are generally less expensive than response lists, costing between $40 and $70 per 1,000 vs. $90 to $150 per 1,000 for response lists.

Response lists are the better choice if you need to cover an entire market of prospects with similar characteristics. For example, if you are selling a service or product to every dentist in the area, there are lists available from publications that serve these markets. Response lists usually produce higher response rates, thus justifying the higher price.

In-House vs. Full-Service Mailing House

The largest single expense of your direct mailing program will be postage. This will account for almost one-third of the total costs of a direct-mail campaign. Your other costs — the mailing list, printing, designing, copywriting and fulfillment — will vary based on which services you require. If you have the resources to do the mailing in-house, you can save money by organizing and sending the materials from your office. Otherwise, a full-service mailing house will do all the work for you.

Preparing for, creating and doing a mailing is very labor-intensive. Consider a mailing of 10,000 envelopes. Even if you have employees that are efficient, the process of folding, stuffing, addressing and stamping all of those units will take its toll. Direct-mail services have the expensive addressing and mailing equipment that automates these and other processes, giving them significant economies of scale.

One more thing: The four-color postcard is the simplest and most common form of direct marketing. It's also the least-expensive and easiest to mail. Other forms of direct marketing such as mailers, brochures, newsletters and catalogs can raise your costs considerably.

Selecting a Direct-mail Company

There are numerable choices when it comes to selection of a direct-marketing company. The deciding factor for you should be based upon how well they deliver customer service. You want to deal with a company that will meet your needs, deliver a quality product timely and is easy to contact when you need them to be available for your questions or concerns.

I suggest that you not be drawn in to dealing with the new kid on the block. Experience goes a long way in the direct mail industry. I personally would not consider doing business with anyone in business less than 10 years. These types of vendors know where to find the best discounts, whether it's during the presorting process or by using a printing method that uses two colors rather than four without quality loss.

Contact several vendors before you do business with anyone. Find out what each direct-mail company offers and then compare all of their services and prices before making a decision. In particular, learn what services they provide to help maximize your response rates. Never select a vendor based on price alone. If the price seems too good to be true, it is. Don't risk getting stuck with a junk mailing list or amateurish design and copy.

As with any other purchase for your business, get references from direct-mail companies before making your final decision. This is a great opportunity to find out what kind of experience another business had with the vendor. If possible, request references of clients in businesses similar to yours.

Newspaper Advertising

Why Advertise in Newspapers?

Immediate response to your ad. If you use a coupon, it also takes on a direct-marketing function. Retailers and service companies that are looking for an immediate response to the services and products that they offer may find this medium worthy of consideration.

You can target ad placement by section in major newspapers. If you are offering a lawn service, for example, you would want to consider advertising in the home and garden section.

You can test this medium with a small ad in papers in smaller markets. Larger papers in larger markets can be expensive to test. For instance, buying a newspaper ad in the Los Angeles Times will run you about $70,000 for a full-run, full-page black-and-white ad. If you live in a small town and advertise in your local newspaper, advertising costs really drop in comparison to the bigger national publications. A full-page local newspaper ad might run $1,000 in your community.

Flexibility in timing of ads to coordinate with offers. If you have a business that is seasonal, you can use newspaper ads

Calculating ROI On Direct Mail Programs

Note: This particular program is based on a mailing done by a service company to 10,000 targeted customers, in selected zip codes, with a projected lead response rate of 1 percent.

Number of pieces you will mail:	10,000
Total cost of the mailing:	$5,500
Percentage of response you expect:	1%
Percentage of those respondents you expect will buy:	50%
Amount each respondent will spend:	$400
Number of responses:	100
Cost per response:	$55
Number of buyers: *(Some annual service/some one-time service)*	50
Cost per buyer:	$110
Cost per piece:	$0.55
Total revenue:	$20,000
Initial Return on Investment (ROI):	263%
Number of customer's renewing annually for four additional years: *(Does not include price increases, referrals or add-on services)*	5/50
Amount of additional income (4 years)	$8,000 ($400 x 5 x 4)
Total life-time revenue since campaign inception:	$28,000
Total Return on Investment (ROI):	409%

to target your customer exactly when the demand peaks. For instance, a pest management company could design an ad and have it ready to go as soon as termite swarming season begins.

Calculating the Cost of a Newspaper Ad

All major newspapers calculate their rates by the column inch. They charge a set dollar fee per column inch. When a publication quotes you its rate, it's usually quoting the cost of a unit of advertising, that is, what a box one column wide and 1 inch deep costs. When calculating the rates for a display ad, it is necessary to determine the number of column inches in the ad. To do this, multiply the number of columns wide by the number of inches deep.

No. of columns x No. of vertical inches x Rate per inch = Total ad price

Let me give you an example of how to use the formula. Let's say that you would like your ad to be 10 inches high and three columns wide. The price per column inch is $20. Using the above formula, the cost of the ad would be $600.

3 columns wide **x 10** vertical inches **x $20/** per column inch = **$600** (total ad price).

Newspaper Ad Discounts

There are typically three types of rates offered:

1. Open Rate: This is the rate charged for a one-at-a-time advertisement without discounts. This is also referred to as the non-contract rate.

2. Bulk Space Contract: This discount is for a commitment to a specific number of advertising column inches within a specified time period. For instance, if you would promise to place 400 inches of advertising in the newspaper during the next year, your per-inch rate would be lower than if you ran one ad one time that year.

3. Frequency Discount: This rate offers the best discount. By signing this contract, you commit to running a minimum size ad each and every week for a 52-week period, although some newspapers also offer 13- and 26-week commitments. Some smaller local newspapers offer even shorter-term commitment discounts.

Designing an Effective Newspaper Ad

There are four basic rules to follow when designing your newspaper ad: Get the readers attention, generate interest in the ad, create desire for your product or service and finally call for the potential customer to take action.

The Headline

Your headline could stress a major benefit you are offering, announce a new product or service, make a unique offer, or create a sense of urgency. It should be bold and inviting.

The Body

The ad should be attractive, contain graphics to gain attention (people work best), have a good amount of white space (not be cluttered), state your message and benefits clearly and succinctly and finally and most importantly, move the reader to take action. Coupons are very effective as part of newspaper ads.

Contact Information

Make certain to include all of your contact information in your ad, including your physical address, phone number and email address. Never use a P.O. Box in any ad of any kind. It undermines the sense of permanence and trust that you are trying to establish.

4 Steps to Designing a Good Newspaper Ad

1. Get their attention
2. Generate interest
3. Create desire
4. Call for action

Some Useful Newspaper Ad Tips

1. Go for size over color.
2. White space attracts; clutter detracts.
3. Use callouts, reverses and bursts.
4. Coupons rule.

Magazines
8 Reasons for Advertising in Magazines

1. Magazines provide the credibility that a lot of other mediums don't.
2. Consumers tend to trust and value what they read in magazines more, and that includes the advertising.
3. The magazine medium also offers a wide selection of segmented venues through targeted titles. This permits the advertiser to hone in on the demographics, lifestyles and interests of the readers and their needs.
4. Magazine readers tend to be among the biggest spenders along product lines.
5. Consumers refer to magazines multiple times — even saving them — giving advertisers the opportunity for multiple exposures.
6. Print offers exposure even when potential customers aren't looking for the advertisers. By contrast, with the Internet, customers will respond to an advertiser only if they have made the effort to seek it out.
7. The magazine gives readers a chance to study the benefits of an advertised product or service at their leisure.
8. Readers usually commit themselves to sitting down and looking through a magazine for an extended period.

Determining "Readership" Figures

When you consider advertising in a magazine, it is important to understand exactly how much of your potential target audience is actually reading the magazine.

A magazine might tell you that your ad will reach 100,000 readers, but in actuality they may only print 50,000 copies each month. Of those 50,000 copies, 15,000 may go to dealers or newsstands. That only leaves 35,000 paid subscribers.

You are probably thinking to yourself, "How will I reach 100,000 readers with only 50,000 copies printed?

Some magazines determine their readership figures and advertising rates based upon their "pass-along" rate. That is an estimation of how many additional people will read the magazine (in addition to the subscriber or original purchaser).

Other magazines base their advertising rates on their distribution numbers. Many times these numbers include complimentary subscriptions mailed out to various businesses, people and institutions.

The reason that you need to become aware of these creative accounting measures is because there is a good chance that this ancillary readership is not part of your targeted audience. Therefore, you are paying for something that you are not getting.

It is my recommendation, when con-sidering purchasing advertising space in a magazine, that you request the number of paid subscribers.

You can also ask whether they are audited by the ABC (Audit Bureau of Circulations). If they are, request a copy of their independent audit figures.

Media Kits

Whenever you consider advertising in a magazine, ask them to provide you with a media kit. I probably didn't mention this before, but you should really request a kit from every major media source with whom you are dealing.

A standard media kit will include:

• A sample issue of the magazine.
• An editorial calendar highlighting specific stories and issues in which you might want to focus your advertising, press release and public-relations opportunities.
• A rate card explaining the advertising rates, allowable discounts, positioning and similar information.
• Advertising specifications listing the dimensions for the different ad sizes, what is needed for black-and-white and color photographs, and similar statistics.
• Circulation information, which depending on the magazine, may be nothing more than a cover letter stating the number of readers. With most magazines, however, this information will be a little more detailed. You will find demographics on the readers and other statistical information.

Ad Placement

Yes, of course placement matters — and in some magazines you can have some control over this. For display ads, you may be able to request far forward right, for instance. You may also be able to request position near the front of the magazine. If the magazine allows this positioning, it will usually charge a premium for between 10 percent and 20 percent more than the ad cost.

Reducing Your Magazine Ad Costs

• If you are not placing your ad through an advertising agency, ask for an in-house agency discount. This is normally 10 percent to 15 percent off of the rate card. Of course, you will have to submit your own camera-ready ad. Most magazines will accept an ad printed with a laser printer or ink jet printer as camera-ready, as well as PDFs.
• As with newspapers, there is a frequency discount for multiple runs.
• Many times, there's a new-advertiser discount if you have never run in the magazine before. Make sure you ask about this.
• Always ask for a discount. Many things could influence a decrease in your rate, including competitive magazine rates or general economic softening.

Magazine Ad Design Tips

• Target the message directly to your customer.
• Make a compelling offer.
• Use a coupon.
• Use photographs rather than line drawings.
• Use people in your ad.
• Your headline should draw in the reader.
• Use a call to action.
• Stress the benefits, not the features.
• Leave enough white space.

Broadcast Media: Radio & Television
The Impact of Broadcast Media

Radio and TV advertising are two of the most effective advertising media that you can choose. However, you must be able to afford them in your budget. These media

are particularly sensitive to repetition. Unless you can dedicate a minimum of a few months of commercial exposure, it is highly unlikely that you will do well with either medium.

Determining Placement Cost of Commercials

When you give a description of your budget and targeted customer profile to the advertising sales representatives, you should receive proposals outlining the reach (the percentage of your audience the proposed programming will attract) and frequency (the average number of times your audience will be exposed to your message) they'll deliver. The costs of your spots will be based upon the number of impressions that you are making, in addition to the time periods that your commercials are running, and finally the number of weeks your program runs (13 weeks, 26 weeks, etc.). Another major factor in the cost of your campaign will be the length of your spots (30 or 60 seconds or crawl lines).

Advantages of Advertising on Radio
- Production costs are low or free.
- You can reach a targeted audience.
- It's a personal medium (people can listen at work, at home, in cars).
- There is predictable repetition (people listen the same time each day to same programs).
- You can reach large numbers of people in a short period of time.

Disadvantages of Advertising on Radio
- Listeners cannot go back to your ads to go over important points.
- You may have to advertise simultaneously on several stations to reach your target

audience because radio listeners are spread over many stations.

Targeted Radio Formats
In most markets, there are local talk shows with homegrown personalities. Radio can be most effective when used in this manner. If you own a home inspection company, for example, I would consider sponsoring the weekly home and garden show during the spring and summer.

Advantages of Advertising on TV
- Has the greatest impact of all the media (visual/builds relationships).
- Ads are more memorable.
- Independent stations and cable offer new opportunities to pinpoint local audiences.
- You can reach large numbers of people in a short period of time.
- As an image-building and visual medium, it offers the ability to convey your message with sight, sound and motion.

Disadvantages of Advertising on TV
- Relatively expensive in terms of creative, production and airtime costs.
- Requires multiple exposures for the ad to make an impact.

Cable TV: The Small Businessperson's Pathway to Growth

Cable TV is an ideal marketing vehicle for businesses with one or more locations in a region and a customer base that has identifiable characteristics. Rates are based on audience size, and because cable TV can be bought in small geographic areas, it's cheaper than local network affiliate programming. Plus, cable TV allows you to pinpoint specific target audiences by selecting cable networks that offer specialized programming for viewers with particular interests. Local cable advertising networks can provide an effective, affordable way to reach qualified prospects who are interested in what you have to offer.

Cable TV spots are usually sold in broad rotators (such as from 7 p.m. to midnight), which makes it more affordable than buying time on a specific hit show. But be sure to check up on your spots to make sure you're getting even distribution during the allotted time — you definitely don't want all your spots to air one minute before midnight, when viewership is considerably decreased.

Production of TV Spots

As you know, sophisticated commercials can be quite expensive to produce. However, if you are doing cable TV advertising, the station may offer its production facilities for reasonable rates. A small business can have a few simple but professionally produced 30-second commercials done for less than a few thousand dollars.

Outdoor Advertising/Billboards:

Under this category fall the following sub-categories: advertising on buses, at bus stops, on moving vans, in subways, on benches — even on tops of taxicabs. You can find out how to take advantage of the mini-outdoor usages by consulting your local directories. Each medium presents significant advantages for targeting your specific customer. For the purpose of this chapter, the discussion

Outdoor Billboard Costing Model

Sample Market: Philadelphia

Location: Highway US. I95 – Near Downtown

Daily Traffic: 57,500 (DEC)

Monthly Rental: $12,000

1. Multiply the daily traffic (DEC) by the number of days the billboard will be posted this month (usually 30).

Daily Traffic 57,500 x Number of Days 30 = Impressions per Month 1.725 million impressions.

2. Divide the number you get by 1,000. (Save this figure; you will need it in a minute.)
Impressions per Month 1,725,000 ÷ 1,000 = 1,725

3. Divide the cost of monthly rent by the number you got in Step 2.
Monthly Rental $12,000 ÷ 1,725 = $6.95 CPM *(Cost per thousand)*

will be mostly focused on large outdoor billboards. Just know that the cost of this type of advertising is based on the number of impressions. At the end of this section, I will discuss some other types of mini-billboards.

Why Use Billboards?

Consider this: A newspaper ad is only good for a day, and a TV commercial only lasts about 30 seconds. But a billboard ad is working for you 24 hours a day, seven days a week. That is one great advantage of having a billboard: the repetition of your message. Usually, the same people drive by it every day. Billboards convey a sense of stability to the customer and give potential customers a larger-than-life appearance.

Obviously, the cost of billboards depends upon two major factors that are interrelated: location and reach. Billboard pricing is based upon the number of vehicles that are exposed to your ad during a one-month period. This term is referred to as the daily effective circulation.

The price of billboard advertising on average can cost between about $700 (very small market) to more than $17,000 per month depending upon your market. In New York City, for example, billboards can range in excess of $30,000 per month. That sounds like a lot of money — until you realize that a full-page ad running for one day in a major newspaper can cost about the same.

Advances in technology have also contributed to billboard advertising's cost efficiency. In the past, billboards had to be hand-painted, which was a time-consuming and costly venture. But with today's computer technology, billboards are designed on a computer screen, printed to vinyl or poster paper and glued to the billboard structure. The result: Higher quality ads in less time for less money.

Today, companies like Clear Channel Outdoor also offer digital/electronic billboards; some of them even rotate advertisers and messages. These companies often are able to handle the advertising for some of the subcategory venues I referred to in my opening paragraph.

Measuring the Costs of Outdoor Billboard Advertising:

Because every type of advertising has its own unique price range and reach, it's hard to effectively compare the prices of each media type.

For this reason, advertisers compare the cost of each ad by how much it costs to reach 1,000 people (cost per thousand, or CPM.) Here is the formula for CPM:

CPM = Cost of Ad x 1,000/Circulation

Unfortunately, the CPM for billboards is a little more complicated. On the previous page, you will find a formula that will allow you to compute what your CPM impressions is to advertise on outdoor billboards.

Other Outdoor/Indoor Signage

You just never know when people will be standing around with nothing to do besides looking at your sign, so consider these venues as well:

- Airports
- Taxicabs
- Bus terminals
- Subways
- Telephone kiosks
- Benches

I'm sure you can think of many more.

Just Enough to Move Them to Action

Remember, when doing billboard advertising, keep your message brief and targeted. You probably only have a few moments to try to get your message across. Just look at this Brock ad above. They are located in Panama City, Fla.

Internet Advertising

First off, I want to state that I am a big proponent of having an Internet presence and participating in Pay-Per-Click (PPC) advertising. That is when you pay to be listed as one of the top headings (positions) in your category *and* when someone clicks on your hyperlink. It is actually a few-line mini advertisement. It works.

Over the past few years, newspaper readership and advertising have declined, as has the usage of the standard hard copy phone directories. At the same time, the rate of Internet usage and advertising has exploded. I fully expect that within the next five years, the use of the Internet as a directory reference will overtake the standard print directories.

Why Have a Web Site?

Why have fax machines? Why have cell phones? Why have computers? If you don't have a Web site, you better get one — and soon, or else you're dead in the water. Why would customers want to do business with a company that they can't find? Most young people (under age 35) use the Internet as their first reference point. Your potential customer will just look to your competitor instead of you.

Here are just a few reasons for a Web presence:

1. It indicates that you are a progressive company that is willing to provide easy access for your customers.
2. It makes your business information readily available to your customers, including your hours, the services and products that you offer, how they can contact you, your location, your payment methods, any specials you are offering and anything else you would like them to know.
3. You can include newsletters, pricelists, press releases, sale notices or whatever information you want your customers (or potential customers) to have.
4. You can ask for feedback and get it instantaneously at no extra cost. An e-mail response or feedback form can be built into the pages and can get the answer while it's fresh in your customer's mind, without the cost and lack of response of business reply mail.

Putting Together a Web Site

I am not going into great detail here other than to say that the Internet is expanding at an incredible rate. More and more of your potential and existing customers are using it every day. The ways in which your site is designed and appears, and its ease of navigation, are a direct reflection on the image and quality perception of your business. While your Web site should contain lots of information, its goal should be to drive the customer to action.

You need to ask yourself a few basic questions:

- Is my home page easy to read? Is it too cluttered?
- Is my site easy to navigate?
- Does it load quickly?
- Do I have more than one topic per page? (Too many topics are overwhelming for the customer)
- Are my graphics too distracting?
- Do I have navigation links that are simple to use at the top and bottom of my pages?

Hiring Web Professionals

My best advice to you is to hire a professional Web designer to create your site, and also invest in someone to keep it updated. While site design can, and usually does, run into the thousands of dollars, it is just as an important an investment as any other part of your business.

Pay-Per-Click (PPC)

Internet advertising differs from other media by enabling consumers to directly interact with the ad. An individual can click on the ad for more information, or take the next step and purchase the product or service.

PPC advertising has become one of the most used advertising methods in Internet marketing. It can be described as an online advertising method in which a business places an ad and pays a specified amount each time that a visitor clicks on it. PPC ads can be easily set up, customized and revised by anyone with even basic computer and Internet skills.

Each search result page generally consists of natural search results and paid advertisements (PPC ads) that are located along the top or right-hand side of the page. Each PPC advertisement consists of an ad title, ad text and a clickable Web link. The placement of each ad is ordered according to the search engine company. Some search engines rank ads only on Cost-Per-Click (CPC) value (from highest to lowest). Others use complex formulas to calculate a ranking of each ad. Ads are triggered only when specified keywords are searched for by a user. Keyword-based searches allow for further customizing by advertisers.

Getting started in PPC advertising is easy and can be accomplished with a very small investment. The steps include completing a simple registration form and presenting your credit card information.

The most popular PPC advertising venues are Google AdWords, Yahoo Search Marketing and MSN Ad Center. Most companies offer national, regional or local advertising options to limit your ad to be seen only by users in the requested areas. Other options may include targeting your ads to specific sites or ad networks. Most PPC advertising companies provide detailed written instructions for both sign-up and for setting up your advertising campaigns.

The placement for PPC depends on who's the highest bidder for their buy (city, county, metro, state, regional, national or international) within the category. It's like an auction. You decide how much you want to spend and bid.

Let's say you want to spend a maximum of $500 and no more than $1 bid per click. After 500 visitors click through the site to visit your site, your ad will be taken off the site — unless you commit to spending more. While it's an excellent way to monitor performance by tracking visitor numbers, it's a demanding program to manage. You'll need a staff member to monitor the program daily, or you'll have to hire a company to manage it for you.

Finally, with all that I have just said about PPC, I strongly recommend that you have an outside company manage it for you regardless. It probably won't cost you much more than you would spend by yourself because they buy the PPC rates at a discount from the service providers.

PPC rates can run from less than a dollar a click in small markets, to more than $10 per click in large markets. But remember, you only pay when your link is clicked on. In the unlikely event that it is not working out for you, you can only lose the fixed amount that you invested.

Internet Yellow Pages

You can also purchase online Yellow Page advertising and optional PPC programs through most of the YP Directory providers. Three widely used Internet Yellow Pages (IYP) sites are: SuperPages.com, Yellow Pages.com and Dexonline.com. The best way to get information is from someone selling IYP. Local-based listings are not terribly expensive, and can

be well worth the investment. IYP placement works very much like Yellow Pages print: The more you spend, the closer you'll be to the beginning of the category. Regardless of placement, if you can't be on the first page, you may not want to buy IYP at all. Many IYP providers also offer performance-based products such as PPC. The placement for these depends on who's the highest bidder for their buy within the category. Advertisers will frequently buy a fixed-placement ad along with a PPC product to ensure they'll still have an ad running once PPC is removed.

Offering Coupons through Your IYP Site

Coupons can also be offered through Internet Yellow Pages. If you've purchased a listing on an IYP site, and have hyperlinks leading to a map or your Web site (or even your Yellow Pages ad), consider adding one that says "coupon" or "special," if possible. The extra link provides two advantages. First, it will likely give you higher placement than some competitors. Second, letting customers know you have special offers gives you a leg up on your competition.

Some IYP sites offer a special option for an icon that reads "coupon" and hyperlinks to it. Others may have a hyperlink on "details," with details in parentheses. In that case, make sure you include information about your special offer. Just be sure that if your link indicates a "special," you follow through with a deal.

Organic Web Site Pptimization

If you are not currently purchasing

PPC advertising, then you are dependent on your customers finding you through what is commonly called the natural or organic search selection process. The field of search engine optimizaton (SEO) is concerned with maximizing the visibility of a Web site by making its listings appear more frequently and more prominently in organic search results. An organic search engine uses a combination of computer algorithms and human researchers to look up a search query. Some things that affect organic or natural Web placements (rankings) are key words and site hits. Selecting the proper keywords and increasing traffic to your site by adding a blog and by making your site more interactive will have an impact on your natural search ranking. The bottom line is that hiring a company that specializes in SEO is a wise investment if you're looking to attract more business to your Web site.

Creative Ways to Market Your Business Using the Internet:

I could devote an entire book to the subject of internet marketing and perhaps someday I will.

In the meantime, there are a few simple marketing tools that I would encourage you to find out more about and consider incorporating as part of your strategic internet marketing plan.

Blogs:

A blog, the shortened name for a web-log (an on-going diary), is a powerful marketing tool that has the ability to attract new business and a like-minded group of individuals (your customers). A blog is an opportunity to control how you are perceived by the online environment. This is networking in its purest form. Adding a link to your blog on your Web site is smart strategizing. (One of my favorites is Frank Andorka's "One More Thing" blog, which you can check out at fandorka.wordpress.com.) By networking and communicating with existing and potential customers you will be amazed at how much additional business you can get. Your blog can also be used for posting Press Releases and other important information about your company. But remember- you will need to assign someone in your company to care for it and respond to postings on a regular basis.

E-zines and E-newsletters:

An E-zine is simply an electronic newsletter that is delivered by email to your customers.

It's a critical business tool to foster and develop relationships within your niche, to keep in close contact with your clients, build your credibility or perceived expertise in the marketplace and drive leads and sales.

Broadcast E-Mail:

Bulk-E Broadcast E-Mail allows you to automatically send the same e-mail message simultaneously (or nearly so) to hundreds, thousands or millions of destinations. This means that now you can send information, such as advertising, newsletters, announcements or even invoices, to any number of recipients virtually simultaneously! Bulk-E Broadcast E-Mail offers you practically effort-free distribution of information at a cost of just pennies per recipient. Of course, when mailing to potential customers you must be careful that you allow the recipients to "opt-in" or "opt out" so that the material will not be viewed as SPAM.

Reciprocal Links with Complimentary Organizations and Trade Groups

A great way of generating potential new business is linking your website to other related or informative sites, such as: trade organizations, Chambers of Commerce, etc.

Maintain a Presence on Social Networking Sites

Sites like Angies List.com, Craigs List.com and Facebook.com allow for additional marketing opportunities. You can do anything from listing your business to acquiring your own page to trying some limited advertising. Each networking group has its own unique criteria for joining and marketing. If you are searching for a professional business networking group, then I suggest that you consider linkedin.com.

Advertising Agencies

If you are doing more than $2 million in revenue, you should definitely consider hiring an advertising agency. At this point in your company's evolution, you have too many things to juggle, and making a critical mistake in your marketing placement or strategy could be detrimental and costly. Below, you will find a few of the reasons to make this move:

• Agencies have relationships with the media and can usually negotiate better deals.

• They receive their commission (a standard 15 percent) from the media with whom they place your advertising, so there is

no cost to you for professional advice regarding the ad placements.

• They have an intimate knowledge of targeting and market share and subscribe to professional monitoring services like Arbitron, Nielsen and the other independent newspaper, directory and outdoor auditing agencies.

• The placing of advertising can be a full-time job in and of itself. It can require hours upon hours of meeting with individual ad representatives and even more time going through the decision-making process. You will save a great amount of time by working with an ad agency. It will allow you to break through the volume of choice clutter that you would otherwise have to deal with yourself.

• You will receive their input and knowledge, and they will assist you in making prudent decisions.

Other Agency Fees

While strategic meetings, advertising and marketing advice and advertising placements are included in the 15 percent commission fee they receive from the media; other charges, such as production costs and design work, are additional. For the creation of brochures and other small items, you may decide that it is more cost-effective to continue on with your current resources. However, many times agencies can provide competitive rates because they deal in such volume.

In-House Agencies

Many times, you can take advantage of the 15 percent agency discount as well if you are doing your own advertising placement. Now that you are aware that TV and radio

stations, newspapers, directories and magazines all give a 15 percent commission off the price of their rate cards to advertising agencies, ask them to give you the same consideration. When you are negotiating your rates keep this in mind.

chapter 17
Marketing to Women

The female market is not a niche. It is an economic powerhouse of primary consumers. Women are not a specialty market; it's therefore important to incorporate them into the regular marketing budget. Instead of just "thinking pink" when you market to this segment, think solid information, ease of use, outstanding customer service, simple design and forming trusting, respectful relationships.

Some Interesting Facts about Women's Buying Power

- Women make more than 80 percent of the buying decisions in U.S. households today, and they influence 95 percent of all buying decisions. They've become nearly every family's chief purchasing officer.
- Women are buying a majority of all consumer electronics and home improvement goods today.
- Women are dramatically changing how products are designed and marketed in America.
- This year, 80 percent of women plan on doing some home-improvement project, and 75 percent of them will do it themselves.
- By 2010, they'll control more than $13 trillion in private wealth.
- A Sears survey revealed that if given the choice of an hour of free advice from home-repair pro Bob Vila or popular psychologist Dr. Phil, 63 percent of women would chose Vila.
- Women's purchasing decisions can make or break brands.

The Demographics

- There are 118.5 million women in the nation's central cities and their suburbs, more than half the urban population.
- About 17 million women in those areas are age 65 and older — almost 60 percent of the total number of seniors in cities.
- Women 65 and older are three times as likely as their male counterparts to live alone.
- More than 14 million women live alone in cities.
- More than 23 million women are heads of households.
- More than 60 percent of those who care for an older person are women.

Focusing on Women Delivers the Best Results

One thing that you need to know about women: They are not afraid to stop and ask for help (unlike the vast majority of men, who would rather wind up in Alaska than ask for directions). Additionally, women are more demanding in their quest for information about any product, service or marketing campaign.

If you incorporate the higher information-delivery demands and customer service standards of women into the development of your product or service, you will give the men more than they thought to ask for.

Characteristics That Women Share

- Relationship-oriented
- Interested in soliciting consensus from a group
- Thorough in their research prior to the purchase
- Worried about the feelings of others
- Value-oriented
- Appreciative of respect and integrity in a business relationship
- Loyal customers

What Women Want
- Service
- Customer service
- Convenience
- Value
- Relationships
- Communication
- Respect
- Information
- Convenience

Women demand extraordinary service, exceptional customer service, convenience and value. Those are at the very top of their list. Extraordinary service involves a sales staff that's knowledgeable and professional. It requires being able to balance being helpful with knowing when to give her space.

When the sales personnel listen to what women want, they need to ask them questions and provide product recommendations that fit their needs. They need to work hard to furnish a service and gain their trust and respect.

Exceptional customer service means being there after the sale is made and delivering more than is promised, at a reasonable price, in a timely fashion. Convenience plays a big part in most women's decision-making process because their time is so limited. It influences how they shop, where they shop and when. Women will pay more for an item if they understand the additional value they will receive in services, features, benefits and reliability.

When Marketing to Women, Remember....
- Create visual points of reference. Women use the right side of their brain more often — the creative side.
- Talk about how your product or service will fill their needs.
- Word of mouth is crucial for women's purchase decisions. Make certain to stand behind your products and services.
- Women generally prefer more detail than men in their pitches.
- Women are not impulse buyers. They spend a great deal of time thinking about their potential purchases, doing research and gathering information. Once they have the information, they will mull over their considerations again — seeking opinions and input from independent sources, friends, family and co-workers. Men, on the other hand, will go from point A (consideration of the purchase) to point B (the sale) in almost a straight line. They may look into a few options, but once men have satisfied the need-to-know part of their brain, they make the buy. No outside opinion needed.

Some Tips When Putting Together Your Campaigns
Involve women and seek their input when putting together your marketing programs. This allows you to create compelling messages for your customers. Pay attention to what women tell you. Ask open-ended questions, and listen carefully to the answers.

- Marketing to women successfully requires a careful consideration of their beliefs and values.
- Identify creative approaches to connecting with the social and community causes.
- Target your customer through your ads by staging her, not by aging her. For example: Create separate ads for the

vibrant age (18-25), the family stage (child rearing) and the retirement stage.

• Reference the mother-daughter bond in your graphics and ads. This is a strong relationship and builds the sense of trust and relationships into your ads.

• Be more concerned with her worth as a lifelong customer than just her transaction today.

• Exceed their expectations.

Quick Tips on Selling to Women

• If a woman and her spouse are present during a sales presentation, give them both a business card. It is a very inexpensive way to let her know you consider her part of the process from the beginning.
• When you ask questions, address at least half of them to her.
• When answering a question she asked, talk to her, not her spouse.
• If a woman is by herself during the sales process, assume she is the one making the buying decision and that she will be paying for it with her money. Take her seriously.
• If the woman tells you that she needs to check it out with her husband first and that she will get back to you, you probably just blew the sale.
• Executives used to spouting orders, or salespeople primed to do the majority of the talking, need to readjust their strategies when dealing with women. Women will listen politely, seeming to indicate they are interested in doing business with you when actually that is not always the case. When spoken to at length, women nod their heads to confirm they are listening, not to convey their approval or acceptance of

the deal, while a man's nod more often signifies agreement. This demonstrates that women and men are very different in the way in which they receive and respond to psychological clues.

To Sum It All up

Establishing a business relationship with women will guarantee a long-term, loyal association, rather than just a one-shot purchase. Women tend to converse more with each other — to recommend, refer and repeat doing business with people they trust and respect.

Relationships take time. Closing a deal with a woman may take longer, but it is well worth the time and effort. Women seek out companies that value them and accommodate their needs.

In this short chapter, I have barely scratched the surface of marketing to women. If you would like to learn more, I suggest that you avail yourself of one of the many recent books on this subject like *Marketing to Women* by Marti Barletta, or *The Soccer Mom Myth* by Michelle Miller and Holly Buchanon. These books are just a start to help you understand this critical market that will help drive your current *and* future business.

chapter 18
Green Marketing

According to The Mintel International Group, a privately owned, London-based market research firm with offices throughout the world (including the United States), about 12 percent of the U.S. population can be identified as "True Green," or consumers who seek out and regularly buy environmentally friendly, so-called "green" products. Another 68 percent can be classified as "Light Green," or consumers who buy green sometimes.

This research confirms what most businesses have already come to recognize: The green movement is steadily and most assuredly lifting itself up from the ranks of the fringe (and what would heretofore be described as trendy) and into the mainstream.

Another recent survey discovered that the majority consumers prefer to do business with companies that demonstrate that they care about the environment. A significant number of the respondents stated that they would pay more for environmentally friendly products and services.

How much more would they be wiling to pay for green services and/or products? That answer varies by product, service and industry, but generally speaking, a significant number of consumers (more than 50 percent) are willing to pay slightly more (5 percent to 10 percent) for green products and services.

According to Google Trends, the research arm of Google, search volume for "green marketing" continued to trend upward in 2007.

Other indications that "green" is becoming part of our permanent culture:

• The news and entertainment media are focusing more on green stories.

• The building and construction industries are producing and selling more energy-efficient products.

• Automakers are manufacturing, advertising and selling more hybrid vehicles.

• National retailers such as Wal-Mart, Home Depot and Lowe's are "greening up" their stores through the use of energy-efficient polices. This includes "encouraging" their suppliers to participate in helping them achieve their goals, asking them to adapt their products (when applicable) to become more environmentally responsible.

• Companies like Disney are making significant modifications to the way in

> Wal-Mart Executive Charles Zimmerman made the following statement during the unveiling of a Superstore in Kansas City, Mo., in January 2007:
> *"It is our goal...to be supplied by 100 percent renewable energy, to create zero waste and to sell products that sustain our resources and environment."*

which they operate. Some of their "green modifications" include: Retooling the engines on their Disneyland submarine ride, "Finding Nemo," which have been adapted from originally operating on diesel fuel to today running on clean and quiet magnetic coils. The fake coral reefs under water are not colored with paint anymore, but with recycled glass sprayed on with an organic epoxy.

• Industries such as pest management and lawn care are offering environmentally responsible products and services, including organic product options.

• Clorox recently introduced Green Works, a new line of green cleaning products

that claim to be "at least 99 percent natural" — made from coconuts and lemon oil, formulated to be biodegradable and non-allergenic, packaged in recyclable bottles and not tested on animals. This is the company's first new brand launch in 20 years. Clorox's testing showed that these products, with 99 percent or more natural ingredients, "work as well as Lysol, 409 and Pine-Sol." Did I mention that this product line just received a third-party, independent endorsement by the Sierra Club?

Up until this point, you may have noticed that I have not specifically defined the concept of green or more precisely, what green marketing is. This is primarily because these definitions vary. So for that, I will refer you to a few interpretations of what green means to different groups and organizations.

According to the American Marketing Association, green marketing is the marketing of products that are presumed to be environmentally safe. Thus, green marketing incorporates a broad range of activities, including product modification, changes to the production process, packaging changes and even modifying advertising. Yet defining green marketing is not a simple task where several meanings intersect and contradict each other; an example of this will be the existence of varying social, environmental and retail definitions attached to this term.

Below, please find three other definitions of green marketing, based on three different segments:

Retailing Definition:
The marketing of products that are presumed to be environmentally safe.

Environmentalists' Definition:
The efforts by organizations to produce, promote, package and reclaim products in a manner that is sensitive or responsive to ecological concerns.

Social Marketing Definition:
The development and marketing of products and services designed to minimize negative effects on the physical environment or to improve its quality.

Now, we probably could get into a debate about the substantive meaning of green. If you are providing green-related services and/or products, the precise definition may even differ within industries, service sectors and companies. But I believe that the one common element that exists within the subtext of all definitions is environmental stewardship and responsibility. It is how well you deliver and market these "characterizations," in conjunction with how in sync you are with your customer's expectations, that will ultimately prove your green marketing strategy to be successful.

If you are still convinced that "Going Green" is a trend, or something that is not becoming institutionalized into our business culture, then I would like you to consider how some other fads and trends performed as well, such as fax machines, cell phones, computers, the Internet and the move in the food industry toward healthier foods (including ingredient labeling). Even the exercise industry evolved from pressure to live healthier lifestyles by participation in health clubs and businesses that sprouted up to meet those demands.

The national movement toward green

is not a trend; in my opinion, it is already a reality. Most major business sectors throughout the country have already embraced green initiatives.

Bolstering Your Green Identity

There are steps that you can take to impress your customers with your commitment to environmental stewardship, regardless of whether you are offering green products or services for sale. Implementing these ideas in the workplace, and then informing your customers (through marketing programs) of your company's sincere commitment to environmental responsibility, will do wonders to bolster your green image in the mind of your market.

Here are just a few of the things that you can put into effect in your workplace:

• Use recycled paper and paper products.

• Add hybrid vehicles to your fleet.

• Reorganize routes for better gas consumption.

• Switch off unnecessary lights around the workplace.

• Replace existing light bulbs with low-energy equivalents.

• Turn off computers at the end of every workday.

• Use personal mugs and glasses rather than plastic or plastic foam containers.

• Recycle glass, cans, newspapers and corrugated cardboard.

• Keep vehicles well maintained to reduce fuel consumption.

• Use a garage that recycles used oil and batteries.

• Replace plastic water bottles with a water cooler.

• Provide incentives for employee participation outside of the workplace.

• Purchase energy-efficient products.

• Commit to the use of environmentally responsible products and materials.

What is the green customer looking for?

If you are already selling products or services to the green market, be particularly aware that focusing on the following areas are extremely important.

Results: No matter the product or service that you are offering to the green target market, the customer's first priority is results. While consumers care deeply about environmental impact, research shows that their first priority is solving their problem. If you are in a business segment that is considering modification of your product or service line to include green products, only make the transition if your company can equal or surpass your current service delivery system or product offerings. If you are in a service industry, offer supplementary green service options — with your current product and service lines as a backup if necessary.

Safety/Peace of Mind/Social

Responsibility: After results, the safety consideration of the product or service being delivered is crucial to the customer. Customers who choose to purchase green products and services do so because they believe that they are safer and leave less of a footprint on the environment. Therefore, three needs and desires are fulfilled at once: safety, peace of mind and their personal sense of social responsibility.

Credibility: Deliver what you promise and promise only what you can deliver. If you make a claim that your new green product

or service will perform equal to or above your current service/or product line, you had better be able to back up that claim with results or your credibility will be seriously damaged.

Communication: Communication is crucial when informing current or prospective customers about green products or services. If you are adding a new green product or service line, make certain to state the benefits over your existing product or service offerings. Of course, focus on the reasons for adding this service or product to your menu — namely, your contribution and commitment to environmental responsibility.

Professionalism/Image: Projecting a positive image and an aura of professionalism is imperative when marketing green products and services. Service personnel, advertising, sales staff, vehicles, appearance of retail space — all of these play a role in your commitment to social responsibility. Both the delivering of green goods and services and the image that you project make up a cohesive and powerful marketing program.

Selling Green Products or Services to your Current Customers

Selling green products and services are not much different than selling anything else that your company offers. In fact, it is easier, because you have the consumer perception of environmental responsibility and the inherent assumption of safety in the mind of the customer.

Green Selling Tips...

• Explain how the product or service will fill the needs of your customers.
• Focus on the value of the products or services.
• Review the benefits of the products or services.
• Make certain that your employees are thoroughly trained in the differences between your standard products and services and your green offerings.
• When offering green products and services, refer to third-party, independent credentialing to add credibility.

Third-Party Credentialing

It will give your company added credibility when you market your product if you can display a third-party independent seal that affirms that your product or service meets the green standards set by an independent and respected organization. Remember how the Clorox Co. attained the stamp of approval from the Sierra Club for its Green Works cleaning product line?

An example of service sector credentialing can be demonstrated by looking at the pest management industry, where the IPM Institute of North America offers members that conform to its standards the right to display its independent Green Shield Certified seal.

I would also be remiss if I neglected to

mention that the National Pest Management Association (NPMA) has also launched its QualityPro Green program, bringing the weight of the national association to this quickly growing market, and I commend them for their commitment on this issue.

Generating Free Public Relations

The media has demonstrated a keen interest in writing about and featuring green products and services. Aggressive companies will create press releases to be distributed to local media outlets that feature the introduction of their new products and services in their market.

Additionally, you can discuss your company's efforts to "green up" your workplace and inform them of any incentive programs that you choose to offer your employees by participating in an environmentally responsible lifestyle at home. For example:

• Organize a tree planting event in your local community, sponsored by your company. Invite the community to participate.

• Offer financial incentives to employees who choose to make green improvements to their home or lifestyle. Offer to reimburse the employee up to a set amount per year for home improvements like the addition of insulation, the purchase of energy-efficient windows or the purchase of hybrid vehicles.

Imagine the story about your business that could appear in your local newspaper with the following headline, generated from the press release that you have sent out:

Local Company Goes Green
Offers Employees Incentives for Environmental Responsibility

There are many creative ideas that I am

> The Frontera Grill has created the largest composting endeavor in Chicago, sending food waste each week to a not-for-profit environmental organization that emphasizes recycling, composting and educational programs, and runs a farm in a gentrifying inner-city neighborhood.

sure that you can come up with to generate free press about your evolution into this marketplace. Just look at how one Chicago restaurateur generated massive PR for his businesses.

As you can see, going green offers many opportunities for growth and profit. But be prepared to stand behind what you offer and be a true guardian of the environment as well as a businessperson.

If the customer suspects that your only motive in entering this market is profit-based, your credibility may be at risk.

Epilogue

I hope that you have found this book to be enlightening and informative. I have tried to make it both comprehensive and topical. It's my hope that it will stimulate you into action, while at the same time provide you with a useful resource for many years to come.

I wish to thank all of the individuals, educators, lecturers, authors, clients, educational institutions, sources and resources that I have tapped into over the past 40 years, for providing me with the voluminous wealth of information, material and data that it took to compile this book. Without their teachings and writings, this book would not have been possible. And so, I now pass this information on to you. You are now the keeper of the knowledge.

As I was writing this book, it was a major goal of mine to have you understand the symbiotic relationships that exist among all the different facets of marketing and how they interrelate to one another. Granted, it is a little daunting when you realize just how many parts of your business are influenced by and dependent upon, marketing.

One thing should be crystal clear to you by now: Advertising and marketing are related, but definitely not defined in the same way. Marketing is all-inclusive and permeates not only your advertising, but almost every other facet of your business.

I wish you success, growth and profitability.

Oh yes, one more thing: If you are in the market for a business/sales/marketing consultant, please give me a call. I would like to help you achieve your potential the same way that I have helped hundreds of other companies throughout the years. My clients range in size from start-ups to companies with annual revenues in excess of $30 million.

Here is my contact information:
Harvey F. Goldglantz
President
PCMC

Address:
632 Chelten Hills Dr.
Elkins Park, PA 19027-1332

Phone: 215-782-1150
Fax: 215-635-6794
E-Mail: *hgpcmcinc@aol.com*
Web: *www.pestcontrolmarketingcompany.com*

Quips & Parables

I would like to end this book with a few quips and parables that I've come across over the past 40 years and still find relevant today. I hope that you enjoy them.

On Action:
Do it now! Today will be yesterday tomorrow.

On Advertising:
One picture may be worth a thousand words, but some advertisers believe in using both in the same ad.

On Appreciation:
Appreciation is like an insurance policy: It has to be renewed occasionally.

On Business:
Business is like a wheelbarrow: It stands still unless somebody pushes it.

Business is made good by yearning, learning and earning.

He who has the habit of smiling at the cash register instead of the customer won't be smiling long.

On Courage:
It's all right to be cautious, but even a turtle never gets anywhere until he sticks his head out.

On Dreams:
The American Dream is owning a British sports car, smoking a Havana cigar and drinking Russian vodka on the French Riviera.

Between tomorrow's dream and yesterday's regret is today's opportunity.

On the Future:
More people worry about the future than prepare for it.

On Goals:
Some people dream of worthy accomplishments, while others stay awake and do them.

Your life can't go according to plan if you have no plan.

On Growth:
Knowledge has to be improved, challenged and increased constantly, or it vanishes.

On Ideas:
Ideas are funny things. They don't work unless you do.

On Leadership:
The business of a leader is to turn weakness into strength, obstacles into stepping stones and disaster into triumph.

Leaders are ordinary people with extraordinary determination.

On Listening:
Opportunities are often missed because we are speaking when we should be listening.

On Money:
The only way to make a dollar go far these days is to mail it overseas.

On Opportunity:
Those who wait for opportunities to turn up usually find themselves turned down.

The door of opportunity is opened by pushing.

On Reputation:
The easiest thing to get, but the most difficult thing to get rid of, is a bad reputation.

On Sales:
Good salesmanship is transferring a conviction from a seller to the buyer.

Too many salespeople know how to say nothing. Too few know when.

Salespeople who keep passing the buck never seem to be making any of them.

Old sales reps never die; they just run out of commission.

Musically speaking, a super sales rep is one with a perfect pitch.

On Success:
Failure always catches up with those who sit down and wait for success.

Nature gave man two ends — one to sit on and one to think with. Man's success or failure is dependent on the one he uses most.

There are two elements to success: aspiration and perspiration.

If at first you don't succeed, try trying.

Notes/Reference Materials/Attribution

Chapter 2: Caring For Your Customers

1. *Customer Satisfaction is Worthless –Customer Loyalty is Priceless by Jeffrey Gitomer (Bard Press, 1998)*

Chapter 4: Understanding Marketing

1. *The Service Profit Chain by James L. Heskett, W. Earl Sasser, JR. & Leonard Schlesinger (The Free Press, 1997)*

Chapter 9: The Value-Price Connection

1. *Going Beyond a Positive Mental Attitude by Rich "Mr. Pos" Wilkens (POS Publications, Shepardsville, KY. 1993)*

Chapter 11: Buying & Selling

1. *Going Beyond a Positive Mental Attitude by Rich "Mr. Pos" Wilkens (POS Publications, Shepardsville, KY. 1993)*

2. *Marketing Magic by Don Debelak (Bob Adams, Inc. Holbrook, MA. 1994)*

3. *Top Gun Selling: The New Science of Ethical Persuasion- by Scott Magnacca, Mark Magnacca and Dr. Donald Moine (article appeared in "The Bridge" Newsletter – Feb, 1994)*

Chapter 12: Take A "SWOT" at Your Business

1. *SWOT Analysis (Internet article) by Anthony Danca www.stfrancis.edu/ba/ghkickul/stuwebs/btopics/works/swot.htm*

2. *How to Perform a SWOT Analysis (Internet article) by Tim Berry www.articles.bplans.com/index.php/business-articles/marketing-a-business/how-to-perform-swot-analysis*

3. *SWOT Analysis ©1995-2008 (Internet article) by Alan Chapman– www.businessballs.com*

4. *A Business Owner's Secret Weapon: SWOT Analysis (Internet article) by Darrell Zahorsky www.sbinformation.about.com/cs/bestpractices/a/swot.htm*

Chapter 13: The Marketing Plan

1. *Preparing a Marketing Plan (Internet article) John P. Camey, Ph.D. www.busn.ucok.edu/jcamey/Documents/preparing%20A%20marketing%20plan.pdf*

Chapter 15: Vertical Marketing

1. *Vertical Marketing Works –The Numbers Prove It (Internet article) by Olin Thompson, Process ERP Partners www.sterlinghoffman.com/newsletter/articles/article275.html*

2. *Vertical Marketing (Internet article) by Sharon Housley of NotePage, Inc. www.softwaremarketingresource.com/article6.html*

Chapter 17: The Media & The Message

1. *The Guerrilla Marketing Handbook by Jay Levinson & Seth Godin (Houghton Mifflin Company –Boston/New York, 1994)*

2. *Choosing the Right Advertising Medium for Your Small Business (Internet article) by Lyve Alexis Pleshette, www.powerhomebiz.com/vol118/admediums.htm*

3. *Cable Ready (Internet article) by Kim T. Gordon, BNET www.findarticles.com/p/articles/mi_m0DTI/is_3_29/ai_72294291*

4. *Consumer Usage of Newspaper Advertising 2006 (Internet article) by MORI Research/for Newspaper Association of America. www.naa.org/~/media/36172C7F3A134293B64ADBE073715EE6.ashx*

5. *Mailing List Boot Camp (Internet article) by Wilson Zehr, CEO/Cendix www.zairmail.com/articles/Mailing_List_Boot_Camp.asp*

6. *How To Measure Your Direct Mail Campaign's Success Using Return On Investment Tools (Internet article) by Wilson Zehr, CEO/Cendix www.zairmail.com/articles/Direct_Mail_Return_On_Investment_Tools.pdf*